The Spanish *intelligentsia* was decidedly inclined to the Protestant Reformation until 1559, when the brutal repression of the Inquisition began. The Reformation disappeared from Spain and its Vice-royalties altogether, and the works of the Protestants were either burnt by the Inquisition or remained in obscurity for a long period of time. That is why the effort of the Cántaro Institute in publishing the works of the Spanish Reformers is worthy of great praise. The present volume contains the *Exposition of the First Psalm of David* by Dr. Constantino Ponce de la Fuente, a humanist who, after serving as chaplain to Charles V, ended up in a dungeon where he died. Even though he cannot be considered a Lutheran (or Calvinist), his preaching and writings contributed to opening the doors in Spain to the study of the Bible.

DR. ADOLFO GARCÍA DE LA SIENRA (Ph.D.), Research Professor of the Institute of Philosophy at the Universidad Veracruzana, Mexico

What a blessing that Rev. Steven R. Martins and Cántaro Publications have made this great martyr of the Spanish Reformation accessible to us. Constantino Ponce de la Fuente helps us gain a broader and deeper understanding of how the Reformation crossed borders, cultures, and languages, bringing the faithful preaching of the Word of God into the most dangerous places, where the Reformation meant certain martyrdom. This is a timely series for this generation as it invites us to stand firm in seeking the continual reformation of the church through the Word of God in our own cities and languages. *"Bienaventurado aquel varón.... [que] su voluntad [es] empleada en la ley del Señor, y en la ley de El pensara de dia y de noche."*

REV. JOSÉ PORTILLO, Executive Director of Hispanic Leadership Initiative (HLI), Planter and Pastor of Vive Charlotte Church, PCA, USA

Constantino Ponce de la Fuente has left for us a spiritually enriching series of sermons on Psalm 1. His meditative exegesis shows forth a unique confluence of Scholastic structure, Scriptural sentiment, devotional tenor, Reformed theology, and Biblical vocabulary. Given the Iberian Peninsula's restricted intellectual environment, Ponce de la Fuente necessarily operated with a Catholic ecclesiology—even though he trained himself on Biblical truth by secretly reading forbidden titles in Reformed theology! In Ponce de la Fuente, Luther and Calvin have their Spanish spokesman who models the possibilities of a "Reformed Catholicism" which might be harder to find in the Reformations of Northern Europe. Martins has translated a valuable work from the Spanish Reformation.

RUSSELL GALLOWAY, Spanish Literature PhD Student, The University of Alabama, USA

Though little-known today, the Spanish protestant reformer Constantino Ponce de la Fuente (1502–1560) earned the admiration of many during his time, not only for his learning (proficient in Hebrew, Greek, and Latin), but more so for his preaching. "God endowed him," said P. A. Rodriguez, "with the gift of eloquence to such an extent that people would flood the churches from as early as four and three in the morning to hear him speak." And as can be seen in his *Exposition of the First Psalm of David* (1546), which contains six sermons based respectively on the six verses of Psalm 1, his preaching was evangelical in theology, appealing to the common people (departing from the scholastic standard), and discriminatory in delivery (addressing both unbelievers and believers, distinguishing the difference between them). A valuable contribution to the study of the sixteenth-century Spanish reformation, his work deserves a wide readership. Cántaro Institute is to be commended and thanked for making his volume accessible to us.

DR. BRIAN G. NAJAPFOUR, PhD, Theological University of Apeldoorn, a Filipino-born American author of several books, including *Joseph Hart (1712–1768), Eighteenth-Century Hymnody, and the British Evangelical Movement*

Constantino Ponce de la Fuente delivers God's Word with a beauty and goodness that make its truth not just persuasive, but delightful and wondrous. Ponce de la Fuente conveys a deeply biblical understanding of the promises of God, and how these transform the desires, decisions, and habits of those who believe in Christ for salvation. His whole explanation, and particularly his contrast of the hearts of the righteous and the wicked, is deeply Reformed. These are truly spiritual sermons on Psalm 1, accessible to readers of every level, and the English translation of Cántaro

Institute founder Steven R. Martins is superb. Ponce de la Fuente helps us take God's Word to heart, personally. I have already commended this work to others and I will reread it as often as I can. You will be blessed in reading it.

DR. THEODORE G. VAN RAALTE, PhD, Professor of Ecclesiology, Canadian Reformed Theological Seminary, Hamilton, Ontario, Canada

As a native Spanish speaker, a passionate lover of the language, and an heir of the Protestant Reformation, it is especially exciting to see the work that Rev. Steven R. Martins and the Cántaro Institute are doing in recovering and reproducing works that would otherwise have been forgotten in the annals of history. Although the present work cannot be called strictly Reformed, it definitely served to shed a light on a dark period in the history of Spain, where, despite all efforts to extinguish all traces of the Reformation movement, the Lord, in His providence, raised up men like Constantino Ponce de la Fuente, who sought to honour the Scriptures and preach them faithfully. In that effort, he became a friend of the Reformation and an ancestor of all Spanish-speakers who have embraced the biblical and historical faith. Thank you, Cántaro Institute, for keeping alive this otherwise unknown but highly enriching part of our heritage.

REV. DANIEL J. LOBO, Translator and Editor for Ligonier Ministries in Spanish, Planter and Pastor of Iglesia Presbiteriana y Reformada Sola Gratia, in San José, Costa Rica

VOLUME 27

THE OLD SPANISH REFORMERS

EXPOSITION OF THE FIRST PSALM OF DAVID

VOLUME 27

THE OLD
SPANISH
REFORMERS

EXPOSITION OF THE
FIRST PSALM OF DAVID

CONSTANTINO PONCE DE LA FUENTE

GENERAL EDITOR
Steven R. Martins

cántaro
publications

cantaroinstitute.org

The Old Spanish Reformers, Vol. 27: Exposition of the First Psalm of David
Translated by Steven R. Martins, from the 1902 edition (Nashville, TN.).
Published by Cántaro Publications, a publishing imprint of the Cántaro Institute,
Jordan Station, Ontario, Canada

Series General Editor: Steven R. Martins
Copyist of the Spanish Original: Sylvia J. Martins
Translator: Steven R. Martins
Book Design by Cántaro Institute

For volume pricing, please contact
info@cantaroinstitute.org

Library & Archives Canada
ISBN: 978-1-990771-66-8

Printed in the United States of America

This labour of love is dedicated to
Raquel Stefany Martins,
my most beloved daughter.

—Steven

The Old Spanish Reformers

— EXPANDED —

Table of Contents

Series Preface

I N THE YEAR 1847, the Spanish scholar and Hebraist Luis de
Usoz y Río (1805-1865) published what would be the first
volume of *The Old Spanish Reformers* (*Los Reformistas Anti-
guos Españoles*), a work that would consist of twenty-four volumes altogether, with its final volume published posthumously
in 1880. This compilation of writings of the sixteenth-century
Spanish reformers, updated by Usoz y Río to nineteenth century Castilian, had not been made widely available to mod-
ern-day readership. Nor had it been translated in its entirety
to the English language. The most recent print edition was a
limited facsimile reproduction in 1983, of which the Cántaro
Institute was able to acquire a complete set from an antiquarian
bookstore in Madrid, Spain. In light of its lack of accessibility,
and as part of the Cántaro Institute's mission to recover the
literary treasures of the protestant reformation, the Institute
hereby presents the first English translation of *The Old Spanish
Reformers*.

Editorial Notes

To the keen observer it will become apparent that some texts
have not been translated, particularly those originally written
in Latin. This was a decision made in light of the importance of
preserving the historic character of the original volumes. Furthermore, Scriptural references have been translated from the
Spanish text cited by the respective writers, instead of utilizing
modern English translation versions. This allows us to preserve
the Spanish character of the original writings. Exceptions to

this will be noted with the abbreviation mark of contemporary Bible translation versions (e.g., ESV, NKJV, etc.).

On the matter of publishing for the first time this series of *The Old Spanish Reformers* in English, the reader will also come to realize that there are more than twenty-four volumes in this current print edition. The reason for the *expansion* of this set was to include those works by the Spanish reformers which were not compiled by Usoz y Río. Whether the documents were not available to him at the time (such as those of Dr. Constantino Ponce de la Fuente, Casiodoro de Reina, Antonio del Corro, etc.) or if he was not able to complete the collection in time is not something we can know with any certainty. However, an expansion of this set with other works by the Spanish Reformers can be seen as a fitting tribute to Usoz y Río and his herculean effort to preserve what are otherwise forgotten works from the sixteenth century protestant reformation.

A clarifying anecdote in relation to this volume of *The Old Spanish Reformers:* This collection of sermons by Constantino Ponce de la Fuente is not the first English translation to be presented to the Anglosphere. The first was accomplished by Juan Sanchez-Naffziger in 2009, which was later published as an appendix to Frances Luttikhuizen's scholarly publication in 2022 titled *Constantino de la Fuente (San Clemente, 1502-Seville, 1560): From Acclaimed Cathedral Preacher to Condemned "Lutheran" Heretic.* As fellow labourers in recovering the treasures of our rich Protestant heritage, we rejoice in and are thankful for what both Sanchez-Naffziger and Luttikhuizen contributed. However, this volume of *The Old Spanish Reformers* is an altogether independent translation which did not in any way draw from Sanchez's earlier translation work.

The Publisher's Intent

It is the earnest hope of the Cántaro Institute that this present print edition of *The Old Spanish Reformers* not only furnishes the church with an invaluable literary, protestant treasure but also sparks within it a reformational spirit and fans it to flame. The reformers sought to bring glory to God in all life and thought, we should imitate them and seek to do the same, guided by the inscripturated revelation of God which is illuminated by His Holy Spirit.

Acknowledgments

The Cántaro Institute would like to thank the Hultink Family Foundation (HFF), the Hispanic Leadership Initiative (HLI), and Sevilla Chapel for their generous financial support which brought to realization this modern print edition of *The Old Spanish Reformers*. The Institute would also like to thank all those who type-copied the original works, those who assisted with translation and editing, and those who advised and aided us in our research. A word of special thanks for this particular volume must be extended to Dr. Ted Van Raalte of the Canadian Reformed Theological Seminary, whose questions and suggestions further refined and sharpened this work prior to publication. This invaluable protestant treasure has been recovered and restored for the good of the church and for the glory of God. And with one voice we can say: "For us there is one God, the Father, from whom are all things and for whom we exist, and one Lord, Jesus Christ, through whom are all things and through whom we exist" (1 Cor. 8:6).

Soli Deo Gloria

Preliminary Notice

T HE EPICENTER of the ill-fated Religious Reformation in Spain was the city of Seville, about which Cipriano de Valera writes in his *Treatise on the Pope and the Mass*:

It stands as one of the most civilized, populous, fertile, and architecturally opulent cities currently in Spain. Its immense wealth is evident, seeing as it serves as the primary repository for the treasure of the West Indies. Its fertility is evidenced by the Ajarafe, home to numerous olive groves which produce such an abundance of oil that it supplies not only a significant portion of Spain but also many lands far beyond. This is also visible in the fertile plains of Carmona and Jerez, rich in wheat, and the fields abundant with vineyards, orange groves, fig trees, pomegranates, and countless other fruits. Even in areas where nothing is sown, the land yields a bounty of asparagus and palm hearts. The city boasts substantial livestock, especially in sheep, from which it exports a great deal of wool to Italy and Flanders. The Father of Mercies has not only enriched and blessed this city with every spiritual blessing but also chosen it to be the foremost city in our Spain to recognize, in our times, the abuses, superstitions, and idolatries of the Roman Church that have long deceived Spain. Having recognized these, it has made them public, aiming for their reformation, so that Christ might reign in His Church.

In this wealthy and beautiful city, the author of this Commentary, Dr. Constantino Ponce de la Fuente lived, preached, spent two lengthy years in the prisons of the Inquisition, and ultimately died. A Castilian by birth, he hailed from San Clemente de Cuenca and was an alumnus of the University of Alcalá. Amid the prevailing ignorance of that era, he was among the rare few proficient in the three languages: Latin, Greek, and Hebrew. He devoted himself extensively to Theology and the Holy Scriptures, and his writing in Castilian was noted for its purity, precision, and vigor. Above all, God endowed him with the gift of eloquence to such an extent that people would flood the churches from as early as four and three in the morning to hear him speak. This popular acclaim was mirrored by that from the learned circles. No one praised him as highly as the celebrated humanist Alfonso García Matamoros, a professor of rhetoric and author of one of the finest treatises on sacred oratory. In his *Apology*, he states:

> Among these distinguished preachers is Dr. Constantino, whose sermons, during his time in Seville, were received with that universal admiration that Marcus Tullius considered one of the foremost indicators of an orator's merit... His manner of speaking was so natural and straightforward, so far removed from the scholastic norm, that his words seemed to emanate from the common people's sentiments, even though they were deeply rooted in the innermost essence of divine philosophy... Much he owed to art, but even more to nature and the rich vein of his intellect, which daily brought forth such things that even art itself, with its persistent toil, could not attain.[1]

Constantino's reputation for eloquence and wisdom was such that Emperor Charles V appointed him as chaplain and preacher, and he accompanied the emperor on several journeys

---

1. The Alcalá edition of 1553, folios 50 and 51; omitted from all subsequent editions by order of the Inquisition.

through Germany and the Netherlands. He also joined Prince Philip on his 1548 trip to Flanders, and Calvete de Estrella reports that Constantino preached in Castellón before the prince's departure, on the first of November, All Saints' Day, noting that "the sermon was as exceptional as those Dr. Constantino always delivers." Furthermore, during Lent in 1549, he preached famously renowned sermons in Brussels. In the *Account of the most fortunate journey*, the same author commends Constantino as "a very great philosopher and profound theologian, among the most distinguished figures in the pulpit and eloquence of recent times, as his written works clearly demonstrate, worthy of his genius."[2]

However, even before his travels to the aforementioned countries and interactions with their reformers, Constantino was already evangelical, undoubtedly due to the diligent study he had undertaken of the Holy Scriptures from a young age.

Upon returning to Spain and Seville from the Emperor's side and the court, Constantino continued preaching to large audiences, which increased further when he took up a chair in Sacred Scripture founded by Master Escobar at the College of the Doctrine for Children. There, he expounded on the *Proverbs, Ecclesiastes, Song of Songs*, and the first half of the *Book of Job*. All manuscripts of these commentaries remained with his disciples who, later persecuted by the Inquisition, took the papers to Germany where, unfortunately, they were lost, with none being found to this day.

Among the many gifts of Dr. Constantino, his admirable prudence stood out, as for many years, he managed not to let a

---

2. The Antwerp edition of 1552, folio 5. The Inquisition ordered these passages and "anything pertaining to the praise of Constantino Ponce de la Fuente, a condemned author," to be expunged.

single sentence or word against the Pope or the Roman Church slip in the books he published with the ecclesiastical authority's permission or in his sermons. The opposition, which later escalated into fierce persecution, only began in 1556 when, following the vacancy of the magisterial canonry at the Seville Cathedral due to the death of Dr. Egidio, who had also embraced the evangelical doctrines, the provisor Francisco Ovando objected to Dr. Constantino's election. Ovando argued that Constantino was of Jewish descent and had come to understand from a summary investigation that "Dr. Constantino was married, and therefore ineligible for ecclesiastical benefice, unless he can prove that he does not live maritally with his wife, and the dispensation he has for it..."[3]

To address the provisor's requirement, canons Esquivel, Ramírez, Fernando de Sauceda, and Ojeda were commissioned. In due course, they presented their report, arguing that Dr. Constantino was not subject to the purity-of-blood statute; since this only prohibited the admission of those convicted, reconciled, etc., and did not pertain to descendants of Jews or Moors; that

> he was a man of very good life and exemplary conduct, recognized for over twenty years as a priest of mass and as a very eminent preacher and theologian... And as such a person, the most serene and Catholic King Philip N.S. employed him in his service, confessed to him, provided him with the Mastership of Málaga, and paid him a salary as his preacher... all of which is well-known.

---

3. See Menéndez Pelayo, "History of the Spanish Heterodox," Volume II, pages 432 and 433.

After a long dispute between the provisor and the Cabildo, and after the matter was referred to Rome, Doctor Constantino received canonical institution of his canonry. However, this triumph earned him more and greater enemies. One day, after a sermon by Constantino, the knight Pedro Mejía, a member of the Veinticuatro of Seville (an old friend and correspondent of Erasmus), "a staunch and zealous Catholic," said loudly, so that everyone could hear: "By God, this doctrine is not good, nor is it what our fathers taught us." This phrase caused great astonishment, as it came from such a respected person in Seville.

The inquisitors summoned Constantino several times to the Castle of Triana, but they could not prove anything against him, and he used to say: "These gentlemen want to burn me, but they find me too green."

Shortly after, the persecution against the evangelicals in Seville intensified due to the Inquisition's discovery of some books that Julianillo had smuggled into Spain from Geneva and Germany. They arrested, along with many Protestants, a widow named Isabel Martinez, in whose house Dr. Constantino had hidden many manuscripts. When the widow's property was seized, as was customary in inquisitorial practice, her son Francisco Beltrán took the valuables to save something of what belonged to them. A treacherous servant reported this act, and the inquisitors immediately sent the bailiff Luis Soto in search of the "treasure." Francisco Beltrán, startled by the sudden visit of this emissary and believing he came not for his mother's valuables but for Dr. Constantino's books, took him to a room and, tearing down a subtle brick partition, showed him the hidden treasure. Among those unpublished works was a large volume discussing *The State of the Church, the Pope* (whom he called Antichrist), *the Eucharist, the Mass, Justification, Purgatory* (which he called the wolf's head), *Bulls and Indulgences, the Vanity of Works,* etc.

Upon seeing this book and being asked by the inquisitors if it was his, Dr. Constantino responded: "I recognize my handwriting and confess to having written all this: I openly declare it all to be true. You need not tire yourselves seeking further evidence against me; you have here a clear and explicit confession of my belief; act then and do with me as you will." They then threw him into one of the prisons of the Castle of Triana, where he spent the last two years of his life.[4] It is said that Charles V, upon learning of the imprisonment of his former chaplain, exclaimed: "If Constantino is a heretic, he will be a great heretic."[5]

There are two accounts of the death of Dr. Constantino, which verbatim state:

Today (the exact day could not be ascertained) Dr. Constantino committed suicide in the Inquisition's prison by inserting pieces of the cup that held his wine into his throat.[6]

And,

They burned the bones of Dr. Constantino because he killed himself in prison with a knife.[7]

---

4. All of this account is based on Raimundo Gonzáles de Montes, page 303, and according to the Castilian edition.

5. Sandoval, *Historia del Emperador Carlos V,* Vol. II, pg., 829.

6. Méndez Pelayo, Vol. II, pg. 438 ft.

7. Cabrera, *Historia de Felipe II,* pg. 235 of the 1619 edition.

These Romanist accounts, far from being consistent, decisively contradict each other. Now let us hear what two of the contemporary reformers say.

In the *Tratado del Papa y de la Misa*, page 251, Cipriano de Valera states:

Dr. Constantino was also exhumed, having been killed shortly before in the Castle of Triana due to illness and mistreatment. This is known from someone who was present. Despite this being the case, the sons of falsehood spread the rumor that Constantino had killed himself.

From *De las Artes de la Inquisición Española* by Raimundo Gonzáles de Montes, page 322, we recite the following:

He spent two full years in prison... He first began to fall mildly ill; later, unable to withstand the heat of the sun in those furnaces, naked, in his shirt day and night, he contracted dysentery and, after fifteen days, in the midst of that distressing misery, he gave his soul to Christ. Attending him in his illness and death was a pious young man, a monk of San Isidro of Seville, captive for the cause of religion, named Fernando, who had been assigned as his cellmate.

We venerate and love the memory of the reformer, and we consider it a great privilege to reprint his works to place them in the hands of Gospel preachers in countries where the beautiful language of Cervantes and Valera is spoken.

In addition to the four pamphlets reprinted in 1863 by the learned evangelical Luis Usoz y Rio, namely: *The Summary of Christian Doctrine, The Sermon of Our Lord on the Mount, The Christian Catechism,* and *The Confession of a Sinner,* we know that he left the following written works:

Discourses on the Proverbs, Ecclesiastes, The Song of Songs, and half of *The Book of Job.*

A large book discussing *The State of the Church,* etc., which, as we mentioned, was used by the inquisitors of Seville to interrogate and condemn him.

And an exposition of *The First Psalm of David.*

Besides these works, there may exist manuscripts, within or outside Spain, of some of the many sermons he preached.

Of the books by Dr. Constantino that have reached us today, we have, first and foremost, *The Summary of Christian Doctrine,* which contains all the principal and necessary knowledge that a Christian person must know and practice. Mr. Usoz y Rio conjectures that the first edition must have been made in 1540. It is in the form of a dialogue, with three interlocutors: Patricio, Dionisio, and Ambrosio. It clearly teaches the doctrine of justification by faith and, far from obscuring the efficacy of works, as S. Menéndez Pelayo claims, it praises them; only it attributes all *truly* good works to our Lord Jesus Christ, who is the Author of all good.

> And do not think that the prayers made by the Church and its saints, nor other good works, are in vain. For when all this is well understood, they are fragments and remnants of the wealth of Jesus Christ, and everything is attributed to Him... and in Him must our confidence be placed. In this way, what His members do or ask benefits through the virtue they receive from being united and incorporated with Him. Hence, you will see that it is a sin against this article to rely on our own works, becoming proud of them, thinking... that by them we will be saints, that by our own strength alone we will advance and please God so

that He considers us righteous and grants us heaven... We must work hard to do good works and services, but also to attribute the effort to do so and the will to do it to J.C. our Savior and King, and to know and be certain that all are gifts acquired for us by His merit... that He is our righteousness, our confidence, our good deeds... and not to rely on anything else (Pages 45 and 46 of Usoz's edition).

Speaking of this work, an eminent Roman Catholic writer says:

> More than the doctrine, what offends here is the tone of the language and the hidden and veiled intention of the author. On the matter of the Catholic Church, he is ambiguous, and when he speaks of *the Head*, he always seems to refer to Christ. He alludes only once to purgatory and does not mention indulgences. The book, in sum, was much more dangerous for what it omits than for what it says.

To this *Summary of Christian Doctrine*, in which he discusses the articles of faith, the commandments of the law, and the Lord's Prayer, he added as a crown and as a heavenly compendium and synthesis of Christian morality, the *Sermon on the Mount*, very well translated and with some very brief notes.

Since the *Summary* was too extensive for children and beginners, Constantino published a shorter *Catechism* in 1556, of which only the Antwerp edition is known, and only one copy exists in the Royal Library of Brussels. It is in octavo and has 108 pages.

Along with this chapter, the author printed *The Confession of a Sinner*, "a beautiful piece of ascetic eloquence, and the most certain proof of Constantino's ingenuity." To give an idea of his style, we transcribe here some paragraphs from that *Confession*:

If I, Lord, had known how little you needed my goods, how insignificant it was for the greatness of your House whether a nothing like me was in it or not; if I had considered, on the other hand, my audacities and offenses against your Majesty, how harmful I was to your people, how much I hindered the glory they gave you, I would have feared your judgment and placed some limit on my sins. But as I was blind to one, so I was to the other. From not knowing myself, it followed that I did not know You either. From not knowing how to value the greatness of your mercy, it came that I did not value the greatness of your judgment and your justice. Hence came my madness and my perdition, because when You sought me with gifts, I became prouder and considered less from whose hand they could come. When you called me with punishments, then I became harder, like a bad and rebellious slave.

With such great blindness, with such great ignorance of You and of myself, with such great forgetfulness of your blessings... my penances could only be very false, gilded with false gold, prepared to be carried away by the first wind and danger with which the devil or the concupiscence of my heart tempted me. If I had built upon You, who are a firm stone; upon the knowledge of who You are, of your mercy and of your justice, all the tempests in the world would not have been enough to carry me away, because I would have been defended by You. But as I built on sand, with a beautiful building in appearance but false in its foundations, my fall was certain, as it was certain that I was to be combated...

I come to You like the prodigal son, to seek the good treatment of your house... And no matter how much my conscience accuses me of my sins, no matter how much evil I know of myself, no matter how much fear your judgment instills in me, I cannot help but have hope that You will forgive me, that You will favor me so that I never again depart from You. Did You not say, Lord, and swear, that You do not desire the death of the sinner? That You take no pleasure in the destruction of men? Did You not say that You came not to seek the righteous, but sinners? Not the healthy, but the sick? Were You not punished for the sins of others? Did You not pay for what You did not do? Is your blood not a sacrifice for the forgiveness of all the sins of mankind? Is it not true that your riches for my good are greater than all the guilt and misery of Adam for my ills? Did You not weep for me, asking for me to be forgiven, and did your Father not hear you? Who then shall take away from my heart the confidence in such promises?..."

(Pages 383-384, and 386 from the reprint of Usoz).

Thus is the entire *Confession* written: it has rightly had, and still has, many admirers among foreign Protestants. There is a very poor French translation by Jean Crespin, an Italian one, of which we saw copies in the libraries of Naples, Rome, Florence, and Milan, and a modern and very elegant English one, done by the late John T. Betts of Pembury, England. His widow has granted us permission to reprint it.

Exposition of the First Psalm. Of the many works by Dr. Constantino that were lost in the 16th century, only this one has been found in our times. This valuable discovery is owed to the very learned and wise Dr. Eduardo Boehmer, professor at the University of Strasbourg and corresponding member of the Royal Spanish Academy. This great bibliophile, having discovered in the Royal Library of Munich a copy of the first edition of the *Exposition*, printed in Seville in 1546, and then another of the second edition published in Antwerp in 1556, published the third edition in Bonn, Germany, in 1881.

With commendable generosity, he has ceded his rights and authorized us to publish this edition, which we are pleased to offer to the evangelical public, and especially to our fellow ministers. In preparing it, we have not followed Dr. Boehmer's edition literally, but to facilitate its reading and sale, we have allowed ourselves to change many outdated and now discarded forms of good language for modern ones; in other instances, we have used notes for synonymy. We also deemed it convenient to divide the sermons into paragraphs, and to verify and correct the citations of Holy Scripture. The punctuation is ours, and for the spelling, we have followed the latest edition of the Academy's Dictionary.

By divine will, within a few months, we will publish the second volume of Dr. Constantino's works. May God grant that this *Exposition* be for His glory and the good of the Spanish-speaking people.

P. A. RODRIGUEZ
Nashville, Tenn., April 1902

Exposition of the First Psalm of David (1546)

Constantino Ponce de la Fuente

To the Reader

H OW NECESSARY the preaching of the divine Word is for men, Christian reader, is evident not only from our many and continuous sins, against which it is the true and only remedy, but also from the testimony the Word itself gives to this purpose. No one can know us better than the Lord who made us, endures us, and waits for us, nor can we imagine a greater remedy to avoid being lost than the one of whom He, who alone can save us, warns us. Since I have spent some years in this highly recommended and esteemed duty with the desire to be of some benefit, though with the indignity that God knows, it has occurred to me at times that it would be good, along with the course we all follow of discussing the Gospel lessons, to include some other things from Scripture, so that with its variety and conformity, listeners might be more inclined to follow the path of truth and see how the benefit of Jesus Christ, the only begotten Son of God, shines everywhere.

The causes and reasons why I did this and why it seems it should be done, I do not wish to pursue now; they will remain for another place. For the present, it is sufficient that I have the example and authority of all the most serious and esteemed scholars whom the Church follows. Among what I selected for this purpose were some Psalms whose explanation I tried to address as well as my abilities allowed. The prophet David has such profound feelings; he reveals in so many ways the ministries and secrets of divine goodness; he is such an admirable knower of God's works, scrutinizing and penetrating the hearts of the good and the bad, the lukewarm and the fervent; he teaches the means for all so clearly that it seems as if the Holy Spirit intended to show a glimpse of the treasures of heaven through this instrument. I do not wish to discuss this in detail now, as it requires more space; it is only proposed so that the motive of what I did may be understood.

Among the sacred books, none is as commonly used or as frequently in the hands of everyone as the *Psalter*. In the ecclesiastical office, most of it consists of Psalms. It is rare to find people of any kind who do not recite Psalms. Nothing could be more fitting, and I have often reflected on this. But when something is so excellent, it is all the more distressing to see how coldly they are passed over, without feeling and without understanding such profound matters. I firmly believe that if the reading of the Psalms, being so common, were accompanied by true understanding, it would be a means to achieve notable benefit, and for many of those who have the duty or devotion to recite them, it would bring great comfort from the hand of God for both spiritual and physical labors.

Of those I have preached for this purpose, one is the very first of all, prompted partly by its brevity and seeming to be properly measured for the occasion, and partly because I have often considered, while reflecting on it, how in so few words the entire doctrine of Sacred Scripture is summed up: everything a Christian must know and do; all the good and evil of men; all the harm and all the remedy; all the favor the good receive; all the adversity the wicked face; all the works of divine mercy communicated to some, and justice to others. This brevity always amazed me, seeing it as a mirror with which both the righteous and the sinner should order their conscience and recognize its defects; the one to gain great strength, and the other great fear. It seemed to me that if the listeners were helped with a copious explanation, they could use it better for this benefit, since they hold it in their hands every day.

The same reason that moved me to preach it persuaded me to publish it. These things easily slip from memory, and few reach home; even less do they last for many years. Due to our sins, it is rare for people to remember the true doctrine of the sermons. If anything remains with them, it is often of little benefit and provides very slight satisfaction, being more pleasing than certain and useful. Thus, it is necessary to support them with writing so that most of the work is not in vain, and those who seek firm teachings and reliable remedies have something to refresh their memory. As it was preached, so it was written: hence, it is not as polished or clear and orderly as I would have liked. The exposition grew very lengthy; however, despite its prolixity, the whole book is small, and from the abundance, each person can select what is most relevant to their purpose. What the Psalm itself encompasses in brief sentences is what is explained, confirmed, and defended. The Psalm and the sermons share the same intentions. In all of them, I endeavored to exhort people not to be content with having a dead faith that merely believes and does not act, for the demons have such faith and it benefits them very little (James 2); it will not benefit the Christian either unless they go further. Although faith is a step for the others, from which the unbeliever is far and therefore more without light, the faith that will save us must be accompanied and kindled with charity; it must be alive and productive of good works; content and assured with all that God says, and executor of what it professes. This is what our Psalm demands, and this is what its exposition exhorts.

I worked to persuade the listeners to have genuine and true charity and simplicity of heart toward their neighbors; patience for their trials; firm and joyful hope in what God has promised; self-awareness; repentance for their sins; mortification of their evil desires; prayer for all their matters, teaching them, as much as I could, true fear and reverence for the Divine Majesty, awe of the greatness of His judgments, and dread of the wrath He has against sin. The Psalm comes down to these themes, and I sought to extend and clarify them by the best and easiest means available to me. We encouraged some to persevere; we frightened others to make them return; we treated some gently, others harshly; some with love, others with threats.

We presented everything to awaken affection on one hand and to instill fear on the other; so that the wicked might at least not advance further and, by any occasion, begin to seek remedy. I have summarized this as briefly as possible to serve as a kind of guide for understanding this exposition, because, with this foundation, the reader will undoubtedly find the path clearer for better comprehension. If at times we seem very gentle and expansive in favor of the good, and at other times very stern against the wicked and destructive of their ways and hopes, it will be understood that this is the right approach for each purpose. The healthy and the sick need to be treated differently. Not all patients can be cured with the same medicine. What seems like diversity is actually great consonance: the Psalm would not allow us to go any other way unless we wanted to be clear transgressors. In it, it is easy to recognize this same variety with the greatest conformity imaginable, which is the characteristic of the Holy Spirit in all His works, who is the true author of Sacred Scripture, with whom everything we discuss in this context is confirmed.

My oversights, regarding lack of proper order or less clarity and other similar defects, partly cannot be excused, as they are natural to my weakness; partly, they can be corrected by others or by myself. There may be things that are so obvious to many that their repetition will cause annoyance; others, due to their brevity, will seem very difficult, and this cannot be otherwise, given what I have already said. Although I understand well that the greatest difficulty of such matters, and what makes them appear most obscure, is how unpleasant they seem to us, the distaste they cause, and our lack of habit in hearing them. We never try what is good, we do not want what is harsh; we seek doctrine that does not hurt us and ask for our contentment in it, as in all other things. It would be easy for me to please along this path, because no one is so poor that they do not find themselves rich in vanity when they wish to take advantage of it; but nothing should weigh so heavily that one neglects to treat such a great matter with a clear conscience.

If we recognized our illnesses and truly wished to be rid of them, we would immediately understand the remedies, because we would feel the benefit. If we delighted in health, what now seems so troublesome would not seem so strange. We look with blind eyes and complain about the light; we crave darkness and claim the light exists when we do not want to be illuminated. Let this serve as a warning for reading the present writing and for others of its kind, if God wills they will come to the light. May He, in His infinite mercy, grant true prosperity to His holy Word: may He give it efficacy so that it bears fruit; so that it awakens in the hearts of sinners the recognition of their perdition; so that they ask for the remedy that is already won for them; so that with a new life, new spirit, and new works, they may testify how they are redeemed with the blood of Him who came from heaven to seek them on earth, so that, as members of His holy Church, they may serve and glorify Him in all things.

THE FIRST PSALM OF DAVID
IN LATIN

BEATUS vir qui non abiit in consilio impiorum, et in via peccatorum non stetit, et in cathedra pestilentiae non sedit.

2 Sed in lege Domini voluntas ejus, et in lege ejus meditabitur die ac nocte.

3 Et erit tamquam lignum quod plantatum est secus decursus aquarum, quod fructum suum dabit in tempore suo, et folium ejus non defluet, et omnia quaecumque faciet prosperabuntur.

4 Non sic impii, non sic; sed tamquam pulvis quem proiicit ventus a facie terrae.

5 Ideo non resurgent impii in iudicio, neque peccatores in concilio iustorum.

6 Quoniam novit Dominus viam iustorum, et iter impiorum peribit.

THE FIRST PSALM OF DAVID
IN ENGLISH (ESV)

BLESSED is the man
    who walks not in the counsel of the wicked,
nor stands in the way of sinners,
    nor sits in the seat of scoffers;
2 but his delight is in the law of the Lord,
    and on his law he meditates day and night.

3 He is like a tree
    planted by streams of water
that yields its fruit in its season,
    and its leaf does not wither.
In all that he does, he prospers.
4 The wicked are not so,
    but are like chaff that the wind drives away.

5 Therefore the wicked will not stand in the judgment,
    nor sinners in the congregation of the righteous;
6 for the Lord knows the way of the righteous,
    but the way of the wicked will perish.

The First Sermon

T
HIS PSALM, which among all the others of King and
Prophet David is placed as their beginning and head,
although in words it is one of the briefest, in doctrine
and spirit is very long and copious, because it contains in itself
all the teaching of what any man who wishes to serve God and
attain true blessedness should do. It also advises what things
one should avoid so that no hindrance may prevent him from
reaching such a great end; it shows the reward and favor that
the righteous expect from God and the judgment prepared for
the wicked; how much the former have Him on their side, how
much the latter have Him as an enemy. If you look closely, this
comprises all the doctrine a man needs to avoid being lost and
to have certain and secure what God has promised him. In very
few statements, this is summarized in the Psalm, but it is fitting
for us to treat and explain it in many.

The Divine Scripture, although written by the hands of
men, was inspired and guided by the Spirit of Heaven; and
although its authors said and wrote few words, a great and deep
feeling remained in their hearts. What we and all teachers must
do is apply the exposition and all the feeling that remained in
their spirit to the brevity of their words; so that, as far as our
strength allows and the Lord helps us, we imitate them in this:
that, having brief words of advice, we have a long and copious
lesson in the soul; much memory is delighted and our will is
enamored. This is what the books of Divine Scripture have over
all others in the world: they are very light in weight, very brief
in words, because they refer all their force, all the value and

meaning of what they say, to the spirit of man so that he may expand, savor, and explain it, and, strengthened for this by the favor of Heaven, put it into practice.

The teaching office is to help the listener for this purpose, guiding them through the principal places and stations of the path, and giving warnings to avoid where they might get lost. This cannot truly be done without God sending favor to both the teacher and the listener. This is what we need, and this is the petition you should ordinarily have in your hearts if you wish to understand as you ought to understand and act as you ought to act.

The brevity of this Psalm in encompassing the ultimate aim and principal purpose, not only of the entire book but of Divine Scripture, has led some to believe that this is why the prophet David, or whoever later compiled the Psalms, placed it and made it the first of all: hence, it lacks any title, unlike other Psalms, most of which, at the very least, have the title "Psalm." This is of little consequence for us, though it is a consideration of learned and insightful men; for whether it is true that David, or some other compiler, intended to signify some ministry in the order of the Psalms, with one being first, another second, another third, etc.; or whether it is more likely that they were assembled as they came or as seemed best to them, without aiming at the mysteries that others assert, this matters little for the present doctrine. Regardless of which opinion we follow, it is clear and established that this first Psalm, in its mere six verses, contains summarized and abbreviated all the doctrine of the Christian religion: of faith, feeling, works, and the hope a man must have to truly attain the redemption and sacrifice of Jesus Christ our Redeemer, so that the eternal Father may protect, love, favor, and bless him. With this premise and warning, we will now begin to discuss the explanation of the Psalm. May God grant us a portion of the faith, spirit, and constancy He gave the Prophet to compose and understand it, so that we may also share in the blessedness it teaches; for he not only sought such knowledge and experience but left it arranged and written for the guidance and teaching of all; and the Lord who gave him this light is ready to give it to us and to all who do not wish to reject it, by whose providence and mercy these scriptures have been and will be preserved until the end of the world.

I have already said that this Psalm has no title; however, if you have been attentive, you can well understand what its proper and true title is, which is a brief definition of the righteous man; a few brief signs by which he is known; a brief guide to the path of blessedness; a security and promise of God's will and help; and a sad end and fate of the wicked, so that the righteous may avoid following such a path. This is the title and the meaning of the Psalm; it remains only to proceed with a more detailed explanation.

Bienaventurado aquel varón que no anduvo en el consejo de los malvados, ni estuvo en el camino de los pecadores, ni se sentó en la silla de la pestilencia.[8]

The first thing we must explain is this word "blessed." There is no nation in the world, no matter how different its language from all others, that does not have a term to signify and understand the same thing that we mean by this word "blessedness." Because, as covetousness is one, and the object conceived is the same, all are equally prompted to express in words what they

---

8. "Blessed is the man who walks not in the counsel of the wicked, nor stands in the way of sinners, nor sits in the seat of scoffers" (Ps. 1:1, ESV).

hold in their hearts. There is no man who does not desire that all things may prosper for him; that everything may go well; that no hindrance may stand in his way; that everything may be done in favor of his interests and satisfaction.

Imagine, then, a state in which a man attains all this, and that is what we mean by the word "blessedness." This covetousness that we say exists in man originates from the greatness of his dignity and the vast capacity that God has placed in his soul, from which arises that great inclination and constant desire to be treated according to the state for which he was made and for which he was given such great disposition. Thus, although he does not know how to ask or specifically point out what will satisfy his hunger, he still seeks in general fullness and satisfaction for that hunger. This blindness in not knowing how to ask, and not seeking the path by which he can attain what he desires, is caused by sin, which has brought such great ignorance that he never has true judgment or knowledge of the goods for which he was created. Hence, as he admits into the counsel and vote of his desires the opinion and covetousness of his own flesh, he simultaneously seeks things that are disparate; some desires for the soul and others for the body, each crying out for what seems fitting, and he longs for all of it. As he tries to satisfy everything, one part leads him one way, another part leads him another, and thus the sinner is never at peace, because he allows himself to be driven by all these conflicting desires.

So, if a man were asked what he desires and how he envisions the state of his blessedness, he would respond with a tower of wind drawn from his heart. In one part, he would be correct, and in another, he would be mistaken; in some aspects, he would appear mad because he would confess that what he desires is immense contentment for all his senses; that he would never hear or see anything that displeases him, but only great pleasure and delight; that he would never err or be deceived; that he would have the highest honor, the greatest advantage, the greatest wealth imaginable; that he would never fall ill, nor would death have any power over him; that he would be immortal like God, and that he would have the assurance that none of these things could ever diminish or change in any way.

Therefore, if a man were asked to express his deepest desires and how he envisions his state of bliss, he would respond with a fanciful construction of his heart, partly accurate and partly fantastical. At times, he might seem irrational, for he would admit that he longs for immense contentment for all his senses; that he would never hear or see anything displeasing, but only great pleasure and delight; that he would never make mistakes or be deceived; that he would possess the highest honor, the greatest advantage, and the most immense wealth imaginable; that he would never fall ill, nor would death have any power over him; that he would be immortal like God, and that he would have the assurance that none of these blessings could ever diminish or be taken away from him.

This is his perspective; however, we have summarized in few words what he would express with many, sparing him from many other vanities he would reveal in his confession. Although the sin and blindness of man are the causes of great folly in these desires, at least it is evident that this appetite, so natural and common to all, suggests that there is some state in which he could attain what he seeks and desires more accurately.

This very reasoning convinced many of the world's wise men to judge greatly and magnificently of the state and condition of man, affirming that he had a certain destiny and end distinct from that of all other creatures, particularly designated for him, in which he would be blessed. It would seem that man's pursuit of this was not in vain or without purpose, for in all his ways, he shows signs of a great lord and appears born for great power. What he knows is a sign that he could know much more, revealing an ability for much greater knowledge, and, above all, he shows great signs of immortality. From this, it can be clearly inferred that there is a state of blessedness dedicated to him, provided he does not lose it by straying from the path.

This argument they made was not entirely misguided, if the lack of true light had not obstructed their path and caused great diversity of opinions, confusion, and uncertainty in their progress. Hence, some claimed that this blessedness and end of man could not be found in this world, while others argued that it could. Among these, some asserted that it lay in acquiring extensive knowledge, and that upon reaching this state, man would be content according to the fulfillment of this blessedness; others placed it in great pleasures; others asserted it depended on different ends. Thus, each one strayed on their own path.

This diversity of opinions arose from the diversity of human desires because, although there are many and they all compete with each other, some dominate in certain individuals more than others. Those who were very eager for knowledge exalted their desire, believing that this was the most natural pursuit for humans and that through it, one could reach the state in which their blessedness lay. Those who were more inclined towards pleasures believed that in the abundance of these lay the true end of man. It would be a very long task to pursue the multitude of errors that have existed in this regard and still exist today. Even if there were no other evidence of the corruption of human nature and the great diversity of desires and judgments in something so important to humans themselves, this alone would suffice. For, if they did not inherit this blindness, their desires would not be so erratic and discordant, nor would each of them make their particular desire the rule for the ultimate end of man.

Let us now bring all these individuals into agreement and concede that all their desires are honorable thoughts of man. However, they must admit that it is sheer madness to think that they can find the fulfillment of their desires in this life in the manner they envision. If they refuse to acknowledge this, let them explain when and how a wealth-seeker can achieve a state of blessedness in this world through wealth alone. The same must be answered by those who seek pleasure through earthly delights, and by those who seek knowledge through worldly wisdom. They must explain how and by what means they will attain such abundance, security, and certainty, without con-tradiction or dissatisfaction, to make them truly blessed. They can only respond with absurdities, as it is utter folly to try to fill such a vast emptiness with such small and miserable things.

It seems to me that these individuals are like the very greedy or the poorly guided sick, who, having a great desire to eat something, say they would be content with a little of it, not realizing that it is madness to think they can satisfy their immense hunger with something that will only ignite and in-tensify it further. Similarly, those who believe they can find satisfaction and fulfillment of their desires in this world are mistaken. They are like a man dying of thirst who spends his time trying to drink from various cups, leaving one and taking another, finding none of them capable of quenching his thirst, while the drink that could satisfy him is in a place beyond his sight. Such a man would be lost unless someone guided him to the true source. The rational course would be to seek a guide to lead him to it. Even more irrational is the person who knows from experience that this world cannot fulfill his desires, yet does not distance himself from it and its vanities. Instead, he should seek a different path, far removed from this world, to remedy his desires, and seek the light to see where it lies, asking for it from the one who has it and invites him to it, for he is blind to finding it himself.

I have dwelled on this extensively so that you might better understand and appreciate the grace that God bestows upon the Christian, by giving him the light of His word and showing him the path to follow and reach blessedness. The Christian can be so certain and assured of finding it, if he does not stray or turn back, that he can confidently consider himself blessed. The consummation and fulfillment of blessedness in heaven is granted to the righteous, but God's Word promises it is so certain that He Himself calls blessed the one who believes in it and acts upon it. Thus, whoever fulfills the will of the Lord on earth already attains earthly blessedness and can be assured of heavenly blessedness. For it is never denied, nor will it be denied, to those who possess the first, nor has it ever been granted, nor will it be granted, to those who do not possess it.

This great treasure of knowing the secret path by which man can please God and be certain and assured of the blessedness promised by His Word is revealed by the prophet David in the present Psalm. "Blessed is the man who does not walk in the counsel of the wicked, nor stand in the way of sinners, nor sit in the seat of scoffers." The first word is blessedness, and it seems that the Prophet intentionally began with it to capture the attention of men and awaken their desire to understand what follows, by presenting blessedness at the forefront. It is as if he is saying: Man, I understand you; your miseries reveal your need; your blindness shows the light you require; your restlessness indicates the peace you need, even though you fail to ask for it. I want to come to your aid and inform you of the very thing you desire; to offer you more than you know how to ask for; to show you where you will find, together and certain, what you seek scattered and uncertain. You desire to be blessed, yet you do not understand what you long for, nor do you know where it is or how to attain it. I will reveal this great secret to you in a few words and give you assurance of it.

"Blessed is the man who does not walk in the counsel of the wicked, nor stand in the way of sinners, nor sit in the seat of scoffers." This term, "blessedness", in the Hebrew language in which the Psalm was originally written, or rather, its corresponding term, has no singular form; one cannot say "blessed-nesses" in that language. The reason for this is that blessedness is a collection of many things. Man desires to be blessed by seeking a remedy for all kinds of anguish and an abundance of all kinds of good. Because God is sufficient to make man blessed in this way, and in Him is found all the multitude of goods and all the absence of evils, the term used to signify this must be one that encompasses a multitude of blessednesses. Therefore, in this context, it means nothing other than the entire multitude and collection of goods that God has created and prepared in the world, which only He can give so that man may achieve his true end and contentment. And it is said that these are for the man who does not walk in the counsel of the wicked, nor stand in the way of sinners, nor sit in the seat of scoffers.

The Psalm specifically says, "Blessed is the man," not because only men can or should be blessed in this way, but to more clearly signify the quality of this blessedness and the nature and manner of the one who would attain it. Although it is true that, in the Sacred Scripture, and in any other manner of speaking, by referring to the principal element of a category, the whole category is indicated, as we see in this example where, by saying "blessed is the man," it is understood that both men and women are included, provided they meet the conditions described in the Psalm. This is a general rule, and there is no need to introduce other subtleties here, which, besides being inappropriate, are irrelevant to the matter at hand. It is true that in this particular context, there is a specific note or indication that suggests we are not dealing with just any man, but with an exceptional one. This emphasizes that to achieve this blessedness, the seeker must be a person of significant action and distinction among others. I express this note by saying "that man," indicating an extraordinary individual.

There are many examples in Scripture of this manner of speaking, where an exceptional man is referred to as "man" by way of excellence. "Are you not a man?" David said to Abner, reproaching him for being such a distinguished captain yet showing so little diligence in guarding King Saul (1 Samuel 26). Acting like a man is a very general way of speaking, and thus St. Paul admonishes the Corinthians (1 Corinthians 16) to stand firm in the faith and act courageously. So here, this particular expression teaches us two things: first, to recognize the great excellence of the one who becomes blessed by fulfilling the conditions set forth in the Psalm; second, the great difficulty in achieving this blessedness, indicating how much diligence and effort is required, and how generous and superior the spirit must be to overcome these obstacles and ultimately achieve victory. We will not delve into this at present, as much will be offered on this topic in the following verses, where we will explain the conditions and laws of this blessedness. This is what we will now proceed with according to the text of the Psalm.

Up to this point, with just these words, "Blessed is the man," the Prophet has aroused great attention and ignited a strong desire in the hearts of those who wander this world, troubled by their quest to achieve a state of blessedness—a state of great abundance of goods and a certain and firm security in all of them. By stating this at the beginning, he signals his intention to teach the path to the happiness and state they desire. He also indicates who those individuals are for whom this message is intended: men of great dignity and excellence above all others, of such spirit and great constancy in their actions that they can overcome anything that might hinder their attainment of such a great end.

Now it is fitting that we listen to this secret, this new doctrine that reveals to men the path to find such great goods—something so desired and sought by all, yet unattained by any who have followed philosophy and experimented with all the goods and evils the world has to offer. The prophet David reveals this secret in a few words. The blessed one; the one who will attain all the goods the human heart, if not foolish, can desire; the one who will receive more than his heart can desire and will be the lord of all the goods that God has scattered in heaven and on earth; the one who will be a man and prince among all men, is he who does not walk in the counsel of the wicked, nor stand in the way of sinners, nor sit in the seat of scoffers. The Prophet promises much by promising blessedness:

he wisely advises what kind of person must strive for this jewel; but at least you cannot say he is a respecter of persons, for he points out a path that is not reserved only for the powerful and princes. Friend, there is nothing of that here. Such exceptions might belong to the blessedness of Aristotle or other similar dreamers and deceivers of people; because since their idea of blessedness is vain and fictitious, and never has been nor will be found in the world, it is fitting that they offer it only to vain and fictitious men, with fictitious wisdom and fictitious power. The misfortune of these individuals will be seen in the other world, and it has been seen enough in this one; for the world itself is witness that none have been more deceived in their desires, more mocked by what they pursued, than the wise and powerful of the world and those esteemed as such.

Here we teach a path that, to know how to walk it, does not require men to exhaust themselves seeking wisdom of the flesh or things invented by human ingenuity. The one who trusts the least in this is the most capable for knowledge: we call both the poor and the powerful, and the poor is sufficiently powerful for the conquest of this providence, provided they bring true desire and true obedience. The rich and the worldly rulers can do no more for this than the most rejected by the world; indeed, it is necessary that they cast out from their hearts the vain imagination of their power; that the wise become ignorant; the rich become poor in order to partake in true happiness.

The conditions of our blessedness are very different from those imagined by the philosophers of the world, and much briefer and with less circumlocution: do not walk in the counsel of the wicked, etc. This is the most common way in which Divine Scripture usually teaches: first presenting the negative commandments before the affirmative ones; warning about what should not be done before declaring what should be done. This method of teaching is very easy to understand and much more appropriate for man, considering his malice and blindness. He more easily grasps how to do wrong than the way he should conduct himself to do right: this stems from the experience he has in his heart, which much earlier gave him notice and sign of evil than of good. Thus, speaking to him of how he did wrong and the conditions of evil gives him news of something very familiar and well-known, while speaking to him of good is dealing with something distant and known only by hearsay.

This proceeds, as I began to say, from the malice of man, to which he is naturally inclined. The senses and thoughts of the heart of man are inclined to evil from their beginning, says the Lord in Divine Scripture (Genesis 6). This is the testimony given by Him who created and knows him. Therefore, since the first fruit and the first thing that begins to emerge from the heart of man are vile movements, it is clear that his first experience and his first taste will be of evil, as something inherently his own. Consequently, the most certain way to teach him will be by beginning with what he understands best and using his own heart as a witness. When the evil has been uprooted from him, then efforts can be made to plant the good and to inform him of the works to which he is obliged, now that his own conscience condemns the actions he previously committed and the malice of his heart.

Turn away from evil, and do good; seek peace, and pursue it, says Sacred Scripture elsewhere (Psalm 34), and the Prophet follows this same order of teaching here, proposing first what man should turn away from and then what he should follow to be blessed. The first condition required is not to walk in the counsel of the wicked, and it is spoken of as something already past: "did not walk," to make us understand the constancy and perpetuity of the action. Here we must imagine that we are judging a man, taking account of his thoughts and deeds, and demanding it according to the conditions of blessedness, for he says he desires and wants to be blessed. For this, it is necessary to say: I did not walk in the counsel of the wicked. By this way of speaking, we do not mean that man must never have sinned, since we have declared how vile his beginnings are; rather, it means that the sin is already undone; that it is as if it had never been: that there is already firmness, determination, and constancy not to walk that path anymore. This is what is meant by that past tense, by saying, "did not walk, did not stand, did not sit."

Walking in the counsel of the wicked, standing in the way of sinners, are expressions from the Hebrew language, which, for what we would say here, means committing sin, being a participant and companion of sinners, following and imitating them. The Hebrew expression says: walking in the way of sin, and walking in the path or course of sinners. In this, it denotes the most harmful characteristic that the sinner has and the most dangerous, which is habit; for walking a path is a long endeavor. From this, we understand that just as walking a path or following a course involves many steps, is enduring, and requires purpose and determination from the one who follows it, so the principal evil of sin and the greatest harm to the sinner is the determination of the heart towards wickedness; the enduring and remaining in it; the forgetting of the offense and treason committed; the becoming accustomed to and forming friendships and companionships with such great evil.

For the one who, by misfortune, falls at some point and, upon recognizing his downfall, immediately weeps for his sin and seeks mercy from the Lord whom he offended, confessing how great his wickedness and ingratitude have been, and emerges from it warned never to endanger himself again by losing such a great good and falling into such great evil, for such a person, Divine Scripture neither marvels nor brings bad news. Instead, it says that the Lord knows the weakness of our composition and makeup (Psalm 103); the vile inclination of our flesh; the great diligence and power of the devil, and, moved by mercy, awakens the sinner himself so that he understands his misfortune; so that he weeps and asks for forgiveness, and He meets him on the way to grant it; to receive him kindly, and to strengthen and guard him more in all that lies ahead. Such were the sins of many of the patriarchs and prophets and other great friends of God, and such was their repentance, so that we may know that, if they had the weakness to fall, as we have, they did not have the malice like ours to despise and persist in their sin.

But that sinner who each day takes greater bait and pleasure in his wickedness and becomes more careless in it, this is the one who walks the path and is so harshly reprimanded and mistreated in Sacred Scripture, and who, with great difficulty, departs from his evil life. Thus, we see that the Lord responds through Jeremiah to His people of Israel who wandered so freely along the path of their sins: "If you say in your heart, 'Why have these great evils come upon me?' Know that because of the enormity of your wickedness, I have permitted your great humiliations. Can the Ethiopian change his skin or the leopard his spots? Then you also can do good who are accustomed to doing evil" (Jeremiah 13). Let us leave this aside for now, as its time and place for discussion will come later; let us continue the explanation of the verse by stating who those are that walk in the counsel of the wicked, so that, being warned of this, we may strive not to be in such bad company, which is the first condition required to be blessed.

Three types of men are mentioned in this verse: the wicked, sinners, and scoffers, or, as we will later say, mockers, which is the same. Concerning the first two, interpreters have worked hard to find the proper distinction between them; who are properly the wicked, and who are properly the sinners. Those whom I translated as wicked are called *impíos* in Latin, and the other term is translated as sinners. These *impíos* and wicked mentioned here are called *reshaim* in Hebrew, and from here arises the question: What kind and sort of wicked people are these *reshaim*? That they are very bad people, there is no doubt.

I do not want to spend much time on this, but rather say briefly what seems most appropriate for this present context. I say that these impious or, as I call them in the vernacular, wicked ones, are those who have great and powerful wickedness in their hearts, which they try to conceal as best they can. Although they do not fail to carry it out in any way, they strive, as much as they can, not to be known or judged as such. I do not say that this is always the meaning of this term in all of Sacred Scripture without any exception; what I say is that in this place we are now considering, it means this. Hence, the action by which they are marked, and in which they primarily engage, is counsel, which is not a public matter but one that has some cover and some secrecy.

Because of our sins, the world is densely populated with these wicked ones, who all partake in a certain kind of hypocrisy, for they always take care to guide their actions in such a way that the world does not fully recognize them; rather, they keep some pretense or excuse. How many of such people can be found, and at every turn; how many wickedly avaricious; how many robbers; how many adulterers; how many deceivers of the world! Given such a great multitude, and given the certain and ever-present danger, our Psalm says that blessed is the man who did not walk in their counsel.

Their characteristic is counsel and deceit, and in all their works and words, they seek cover-ups and frauds. As the Prophet says in another Psalm (Psalm 28), they speak peace with their neighbor, but malice is in their hearts. The prophet Jeremiah describes them clearly, noting their multitude, their traits, and their deeds. "Oh, that I had in the wilderness a lodging place for travelers, that I might leave my people and go away from them! For they are all adulterers, a company of treacherous men. They bend their tongues like bows to shoot lies; they prevail in the land not by truth; for they proceed from evil to evil, and they do not know me. Let everyone beware of his neighbor, and put no trust in any brother; for every brother is a deceiver, and every neighbor goes about as a slanderer" (Jeremiah 9).

And in another Psalm: "They sharpen their tongues like swords and aim their arrows, bitter words, to shoot in secret at the innocent. They shoot suddenly without fear; they strengthen themselves in their evil purpose; they talk of laying snares secretly, thinking that no one will see them" (Psalm 64). Since a single wicked person does not have enough strength to achieve these effects on his own, he seeks companions and accomplices in treachery to more easily carry out and enjoy its fruits. The wicked never have true friendship with each other because each one's ultimate goal is his own interest, and he would prefer, if possible, not to have to share it. Necessity is what brings them together and keeps them in their feigned harmony. For the same reason that they love each other, they also hate each other: they conceal their true selves from each other to avoid being completely exposed; they tolerate each other so that the world tolerates them; they share their profits to avoid total loss. They are so fond of wickedness that, often, just to serve and please it, without risking more, they are glad that there are many wicked people. There are such kinds of evil and such types of wicked people who are so ruled by the malice in their hearts that the profit and gain from it are their own profit and gain.

This province we have taken is vast and includes many people: some as counselors, others as those counseled; some speak, and others believe; some guide, and others follow; some advise, and others consent; some command, and others obey. This misfortune fills the houses, the states, and the hearts of those who, by the world's judgment, are the most blessed. How many remain in the houses of the princes and lords of the world, not for any other reason, but because they serve as wicked counselors and walk in the path of the counsel of other wicked ones like them! From their persuasion and consent come unjust laws, grievances, and injustices, for they are the counselors behind them and whose opinions are their invention and favor them.

In the house of the tyrant, there must necessarily be many tyrants whose counsel he follows, and there are so many participants in these wicked counsels; they find so many who follow their commands and opinions, and whose opinions they follow, that the world is woven and entangled in this abominable web of wicked counselors and evil counsels. One has not even desired something when another, a hundred leagues away, has understood it and put it into action; so much so that they become blasphemers and affront the Divine Providence. There is nothing more similar to Divine Providence. It may seem a mad comparison to you, but if you pay attention, you will see that nothing is more fitting; because many times the worst thing in the world resembles the best thing in it, as we see in lies, which sometimes have a great appearance of truth, and in hypocrisy, which often closely imitates sanctity.

The greatest marvel that Divine Providence offers us, and what most astonishes and even confounds many of the world's wise men, is to see that while governing the affairs of heaven and those of great importance and significance, it justly descends to govern the lowest and most forgotten matters on earth. The same care and order that oversee the movement of the sun, which fertilizes and directs the fertility of the earth; the same power that moves and sustains the great empires of the world, changes them, and brings them down, also governs the lives of ants, descends to the house of the poor old woman, takes care of her chickens, raises her small chicks, sustains them, and brings forth fruit from them. There is nothing so small that moves without its counsel.

In the same way, the tyrants we speak of, who have their seat in the heavens of the earth and govern great matters, exercising great tyrannies, are so well-provided and diligent that they descend to interfere in your small matters, even if you are a poor man living two hundred leagues away. You thought the world had forgotten you, yet a providence, albeit not divine but diabolical, descends from its heights, enters the cave of your misery, takes your cloak, injures and wrongs you, obstructs what you deserved and rightfully earned, ensures the unworthy are preferred over you, justifies those who should not be heard, favors and advances those who harm the world, and dismisses those who bring benefit. And as a providence, you are so troubled and foolish that you do not understand it. It deals with you like a mischievous spirit moving things without you knowing who: nothing is farther from your imagination than thinking that he who manages such great matters would descend to exert his authority and also wish to interfere in the hole of some ants.

And indeed, everything comes and is guided by that providence, and if you do not understand it, it is because it is directed and effected by secondary causes, just like Divine Providence. Just as Divine Providence needs only to command with its will, and then the heavens obey it, the air obeys the heavens, the water obeys the air, the earth obeys the water, and the tiny worms that the old woman's chickens eat obey the earth, without her understanding this orchestration, so too does a tyrant need only give notice of his counsel. Immediately, the entire machine of wicked counselors and misguided ones moves, and from hand to hand, it reaches your corner, where it takes your property or your right or does some similar harm to you, leaving you astonished and amazed at who is moving this matter and how your grievances have been directed.

But if you were a good philosopher, you would trace its course and, starting from those little worms, you would go from secondary cause to secondary cause, philosophizing so much that you would reach a primary cause from which all that derived and from which that influence came: a Jupiter, a Mercury, or a Saturn, for they resemble those from whom your misfortune originated. The truth is, if you were a novice philosopher, you would be greatly astonished at how it is possible that a providence engaged in such great matters would remember your trifles that are so far from the heavens, and it would seem to you that they neither knew you nor even knew if you were born into the world. And in this last point, you would not be mistaken, because for such as you and such matters as yours, it is not necessary to employ so much memory; it is enough to move the eyes, like Divine Providence, so that the entire sphere of the counsel of the wicked obeys, and those wheels of the clock of tyranny move among themselves until they come to strike hammers on your head.

The power of this providence is so great that sometimes to set all this in motion, no more than a little piece of paper is needed. These things cannot be sustained with less, because it is necessary that the one who gives bad counsel and wants it to be taken, takes it when it is given to them. This is the necessary law in the politics of the wicked: no matter how bad the advice may seem to them, they consent and permit it; for they consented and permitted their own, lest they be cast out of the company and shamed, being reminded of what they themselves used to advise when it benefited them. Thus, although they are tyrants over each other, they are also tyrannized by one another, and they hold bonds among themselves, the wicked companions, the wicked superiors, and the tyrants with their wicked companions, so that it is a case of "today for me, tomorrow for you." When one speaks and wills, the other obeys and wills.

This counsel of these wicked ones is the source of the world's evils, and from this arrangement—each one pursuing their own interest and then remaining silent about the other's wickedness, so that the other remains silent about theirs when the time comes—unjust and tyrannical laws are born and originate. These are the ministers of greed, the inspirers of cruelty, the informers, the masters of vice, and the destruction of the world. Some take one role, others take another, and some take them all.

Is there a more abominable advisor than the flatterer? The houses of the great, and even those of the small, are populated and filled with such people. The world has so canonized this misfortune of theirs that it shamelessly says that anyone who does not follow this path cannot live in it. Try never giving or receiving bad advice, and you will see what happens. Unfortunate world, how much better it is to die in you than to live under such conditions! And it is necessary for anyone who knows and understands your laws to be prepared to die and be banished from you; for, on one hand, being so wicked, you recognize the evil you do, and on the other hand, you are so wicked that, knowing it, you tolerate and favor it, saying you cannot sustain yourself without it.

The favor of evil counsel is so advanced that if someone comes with advice for some good, some service to God, some work of virtue, they are slammed in the face with the door and thrown out as a fool and as a lost soul for employing their memory in such a thing. And if another comes with some new form of tyranny or a new artifice of similar interest, he is admitted and rewarded. And even if they know who he is—because no one knows a wicked person better than his companion in counsel—they still do not stop paying him for his wicked advice. Known and regarded for who he is by the counsel he brought, and since they understand that he also knows who all of them are—having taken his advice, with even the most justified and hypocritical approving it by remaining silent and not reprimanding it—they do not dare cast him out of their company or fail to pay him for his wickedness.

I see that I am lingering too long, so it is well to abbreviate what remains of this wicked counsel. In summary, you should consider it established that this counsel is one of the principal kings and tyrants of the world's malice. If there were no counsel of the wicked, there would not be as many and as pernicious factions as you see; no factions so shameless and infamous; no troublemakers so cunning and devious; no flatterers so deceitful; no hypocrites so harmful; no such favor for lies and betrayal; no such bad company; no such dishonesty; no such unjust lawsuits; no such vain superstitions; no consciences so deceitful; no doctrines so lost; finally, no such infamy or such injury to the Christian name.

This pestilence has entered not only the houses of kings and great lords, not only the assemblies of cities and the councils of churches, not only the congregations of religious people; but there are few houses so secluded and lonely that bad counsel does not disturb them. If there were no Ahithophels, there would be no wicked Absaloms to grow proud and rebel. If there were no den of such consultations, there would be no such dissensions among those who govern the State to its harm and detriment. Who, let us see, makes the ecclesiastical prelate choose the dregs of the earth to set as the guide and light of the world, if not bad counsel, given and received time and again? The root of bad counsel is evil interest, and who secures and brings home evil interest is bad counsel: where you see one, be certain that the other is also there. Remove this bad company, and I offer to remove the greater part of the ugliness and shamelessness of the world: at least it would not roam so freely and shamelessly as we know it does in the streets and squares, in the churches, among the religious, and at their altars.

I want to know who sustains the company and league of such abominable men as we often see so friendly and united, if not the counsel that one gives and the other takes? I also want you to tell me: from what does the lawyer, who keeps his door open to receive any lawsuit that comes to him, live if not from giving bad counsel? Where does so much vain superstition come from in which people trust, if not from bad counsel? Where does such different persuasion come from that some want to be saved by one Jesus Christ, and others by another, if not from bad counsel? Where does the avaricious man find the way to be so greedy and to die in it? The knight to be proud and foolish, a Christian in name, but in life an Epicurean? And another to be vindictive, if not in bad counsel? Who deceives simple intentions and makes them, while seeking God, end up in the house of His enemy, if not the hypocrite and mocker, dressed and disguised in false garb? Who harms your children and instills such great vices in them, if not the bad counsel of bad company? Who corrupts the soul of an honorable woman, if not the counsel of the dishonorable? I believe you understand the harm that arises from bad counsel and how wicked is the man from whom bad counsel originates.

But you will say: what remedy is there? Because one cannot live otherwise in the world. I have nothing to respond to you but the same Psalm: Blessed is the man who does not walk in the counsel of the wicked. The Prophet well understood how difficult this is, and therefore pointed out that it must be a man and a great man who puts it into practice. He understood well that the blessedness sought by the world arises for the most part from things that originate from bad counsel, and therefore proposed the opposite view and affirmed that one of the principal degrees of true and certain blessedness is to never participate in or consent to the counsel of the wicked.

"My people," says the Lord (Isaiah 3), "those who call you blessed, they are the ones who deceive you; they are the ones who scatter and blind the way you should have taken to reach blessedness, and they open and reveal others that lead to misfortune." The principal betrayal of which the false prophets are accused is advising the people to follow broad paths of the law and flattering and blessing them as men who fulfilled it (Jeremiah 23). Of these, it says that all the wickedness of the rest of the people proceeded. We do not teach here that the path to blessedness is very spacious and wide; rather, we warn you of the opposite and tell you that what you mainly need to know is that it is very narrow and constricted, and being so challenging, few go by it. Both doctrines are those of Jesus Christ, our Redeemer, the true Teacher of blessedness (Matthew 7).

When the path is narrow and rugged, it is clear what the one who wishes to walk it must do and think; what he must do is prepare and ready himself for the work; what he must think is that he will walk it very alone, because when the path is arduous and narrow, it is a sure sign that few tread it.

The prince who does not wish to walk in the counsel of the wicked must have great vigilance and be a strong enemy of bad counsel and evil counselors. Such was the prophet David, who put into practice the doctrine he teaches us: "Prove me, O LORD, and try me; test my heart and my mind. For your steadfast love is before my eyes, and I walk in your faithfulness. I do not sit with men of falsehood, nor do I consort with hypocrites" (Psalm 26). And elsewhere: "I will sing of mercy and justice; to you, O Lord, I will sing praises. I will behave wisely in a perfect way. Oh, when will you come to me? I will walk within my house with a perfect heart. I will set nothing wicked before my eyes; I hate the work of those who fall away; it shall not cling to me. A perverse heart shall depart from me; I will not know wickedness. Whoever secretly slanders his neighbor, him I will destroy; the one who has a haughty look and a proud heart, him I will not endure. My eyes shall be on the faithful of the land, that they may dwell with me; he who walks in a perfect way, he shall serve me. He who works deceit shall not dwell within my house; he who tells lies shall not continue in my presence. Early I will destroy all the wicked of the land, that I may cut off all the evildoers from the city of the Lord" (Psalm 101).

Let no one think he can escape the counsel of the wicked or the path of sinners without great vigilance over himself to avoid falling into their snares, given the multitude of them on earth. As this danger is so great, certain, and close at hand, the Christian must be so alert that he regularly prays to God to deliver him from it, as something that exceeds human prudence and strength. Thus our prophet prays in many places: "Do not gather my soul with sinners, nor my life with bloodthirsty men, in whose hands is a sinister scheme, and whose right hand is full of bribes" (Psalm 26). And in another Psalm (140): "Let the righteous strike me; it shall be a kindness. And let him rebuke me; it shall be as excellent oil; let my head not refuse it." He calls the counsel of the wicked "oil" because it often comes disguised with gentleness and without fully revealing its wickedness to make it palatable. Great is the allure with which this wickedness seeks to draw others' hearts to itself. Great and powerful is its persuasion, because it coexists with greed, to which the world is more inclined, and with the things it values most. "My son," says the wise man, "if sinners entice you, do not consent. If they say, 'Come with us, let us lie in wait to shed blood; let us lurk secretly for the innocent without cause; let us swallow them alive like Sheol, and whole, like those who go down to the Pit; we shall find all kinds of precious possessions, we shall fill our houses with spoil; cast in your lot among us, let us all have one purse'—my son, do not walk in the way with them, keep your foot from their path" (Proverbs 1). The world is always full of such invitations and offers, some more explicit, others more subtle. The life and conduct of those who live are filled with such evil counsels and paths of sinners, one cannot escape them without great vigilance and care, and without living as if in solitude, even while being in the midst of the world. There is no trust to be placed in earthly friendships—not in father or mother, not in the wife of a husband, nor the husband of a wife—because evil counsel and the path of sinners are as certain among them as among all others. If you start from the high states, from the houses of the nobility, and descend to those of the poor shepherds, in the sacred and the profane, all is corrupted by bad counsel, either giving it or taking it. It would not be so common to give it if it were not so common to take it, nor to take it if it were not so common to give it. How many tyrannies are achieved and introduced through bad counsel, and sustained by it! Let each person put his hand on his breast and remember his relatives and friends, those who loved him most, according to worldly love, and see how many bad counsels they have given him, how much he has been reprimanded and abandoned because he did not follow them, how many have asked him for bad counsel and favors under the guise of good, and have left him because he did not give it.

What we have said is little. A man must also guard himself, for within his own heart lies evil counsel and the path of sinners. When he hears this doctrine that blessed is the man who does not walk in the counsel of the wicked, if he is in the path of sinners, the first thing he must do is examine his heart, for there he will find much inclination to wicked counsel, many actions he has performed and set on a wicked path, giving very bad examples to his brother. He will find such misery and weakness that he will understand how great is the need to guard himself as if from his own enemy, from the evil counselor and bad example within himself. Greatly mistaken is the one who thinks he can guard himself from others without guarding himself from himself. Over both must he watch if he truly desires blessedness. Avarice is a bad counselor, and it seeks great excuses to justify its intentions and actions, deceiving man so thoroughly that he persuades himself he is not being deceived. The counsel of pride is no less dangerous, for the first thing it does is blind the eyes of the one it advises, so he cannot see the deceptions, the vain and foolish foundations on which he wishes to build the structures he envisions in his heart. The wrath and desire for vengeance—what counsels they have given in the world, how they have deceived and brought great ruin to many who attained a great part of the world's wisdom! Foolish and reckless pleasures, and all that gives brief and deceitful contentment in this world, how many follies they persuade with evil counsel! They so enchant the judgment of those not vigilant against them that they make them overlook the manifest bitterness mixed therein, and the sad end where that path leads.

It would be lengthy to detail the great harms arising from the counsel of ambition and all the other secret enemies hidden within our own flesh and house. Not even those whom the world considers very wise and prudent escape these, for these very same are often the deceived and deceivers of such counsels; and they are so often deceived that with all their wisdom they judge death as life, what is bitter as very sweet, darkness as light, steep precipices as smooth paths, and hell as heaven;

and their madness and deception reach such an extreme that, believing and swearing they are heading to the best of these places, they go headlong into the other. This is the greatest punishment God gives to the wicked, particularly this kind of wicked. In penalty for their great stubbornness in wanting to content themselves with lies and give them the appearance of truth, and striving so much to make a lie be taken as truth, the Lord permits them to come to a reprobate mind so that they believe the lie, and the knowledge and judgment of truth find no place in them. Only those who not only live guarded against the bad counsel of their evil neighbor but also watch over their hearts to not be deceived by them, denying themselves, seeking true mortification of their flesh, their appetites, and their desires, and placing all their wisdom in the advice and counsel of God's word, are freed from these dangers. And in this way, they attain the first condition of blessedness, for it is impossible by any other path.

The next condition required to be blessed is not to stand or stop in the path of sinners. First, it was said not to walk; now it says not to stand. It is important to see the difference between the first and the second condition, which can be easily understood if you consider two words in this second condition: "sinners" and "stand". First, it mentioned the wicked; now, it mentions sinners. Before, it spoke of walking; here, it speaks of standing or stopping, which is the same. Regarding this, I say that just as the prophet used the term wicked in the first condition in a particular sense to refer to those who have great wickedness in their hearts but try to cover it up with some hypocrisy, he now uses the term sinner in another particular sense. We find this clearly in many places in the gospel, where the sinful woman is specifically called a sinner, indicating that her sin is known and public. The Pharisee said, "She is a sinner" (Luke 7), and they accused Christ, our Redeemer, of going to eat with a sinful man when he went with Zacchaeus, a chief tax collector (Luke 19), and many times they rebuked Him for receiving sinners and eating with them (Matt. 9, 11; Mark 2; Luke 15). In all these places, you should understand that those referred to held publicly infamous offices, for otherwise all men are sinners, and there would be no reason to specifically point out anyone. This is the meaning the prophet uses here. So, you will see that the first group received counsel, as something more secret and hidden, and the second group is given a path and course, as something public. Of the first, it was said they walked; of the second, it says they stand or stop because those who walk and pass by cannot be as clearly and consistently known as those who stand still. From this, you will understand what I have said: just as the first group were wicked, and as much as their strength allowed, they disguised themselves and were hypocrites, conducting their affairs through deceit and treachery, keeping a facade to appear good before men, the second group are those who so recklessly covet their interests that they disregard all the infamy that can follow from them, preferring to be known for who they are rather than restrain their desires even slightly. The world is not as populated with these as with the first, but it is still more so than is fitting for the glory of God and the benefit of men. How many will you see who are so brazenly and shamelessly wicked that, whether you understand them or not, whether you know who they are or not, they do not care, and will pursue their malice to the end! "The wicked man," says Solomon, "when he comes to the depth of his sins, also comes to despise" (Prov. 18). First, he despised the judgment of God in his heart, and then he comes to publicly despise the judgment of men. This is a great power of Satan in the hearts of his followers, bringing them to a state where they receive no shame from such a disgraceful thing as sin. Many even seek their honor through this, and boast in the eyes of men about being who they are and being esteemed as such.

In this number are many who, with their face and words and deeds, make you understand that it is necessary not to displease them even slightly or obstruct their wickedness, lest you pay dearly for it. And for this, they need neither occasion nor pretense of justice on their part, nor any guilt on yours; it is enough that they want and can treat you as they please, and they will do so and boast about it. The prophet paints these in another Psalm and describes their characteristics so that you can recognize them and know their deeds: "Why do you boast of evil, O mighty man? Why do you boast all day long, you who are a disgrace in the eyes of God? Your tongue plots destruction; it is like a sharpened razor, you who practice deceit. You love evil rather than good, falsehood rather than speaking the truth" (Psalm 52). If there were justice on earth, I speak of human justice and the justice that reason demands of men, there would not be so many of these as there are, because even if heavenly punishment is delayed, earthly punishment would restrain them. But because of our great sins, we see that those we speak of are often exempted and favored, and they despise the same justice that sometimes favors or overlooks them, and justice also fears them. It is a great misery and abomination that sin reigns in the world to such an extent that what men usually fear and value most when they disregard God—the judgment of other men—comes to be despised along with God's judgment, so that neither in regard to heaven nor in regard to earth do they conceal their wickedness. And anyone who so boldly, with such audacity and disdain, is so wicked before men, content and even boasting about it, believe me, almost shows that they do not truly believe there is God's justice or providence. This scandal is caused by such people in the world, as the prophet himself testifies when he says what these think and what they cause others to think of them: "The transgression of the wicked speaks within my heart; there is no fear of God before his eyes. For in his own eyes he flatters himself too much to detect or hate his sin. The words of his mouth are wickedness and deceit; he has ceased to be wise and to do good. Even on his bed he plots evil; he commits himself to a sinful course and does not reject what is wrong. Your love, O Lord, reaches to the heavens, your faithfulness to the skies. Your righteousness is like the highest mountains, your justice like the great deep. You, Lord, preserve both people and animals" (Psalm 36).

These are the words of the prophet, appealing to divine justice for what human justice permits, and declaring how deceived these unfortunate ones live, thinking that since there is no remedy on earth to punish their wickedness, there will be none in heaven either. These and those similar to them are the ones understood by the words of the verse when it advises that the man who wishes to be blessed must not stand in the path of sinners. The one who stands in a path does two things: first, he is publicly seen and known by all; second, he is ready to go with those who go by that path and follow after them. It is from this imitation and company that the prophet warns us to guard ourselves, and in another Psalm, he rebukes those who do it: "When you saw a thief, you consented with him, and have been a partaker with adulterers" (Psalm 50). In this second type of wicked, a new degree of wickedness is added to the first. Because, as I began to say, instead of counsel, which is a secret thing, it mentions a path, which is a public thing, and instead of walking, it mentions standing, which is also public and signifies more perseverance and firmness. And although the wickedness of the first is great because it despises God's judgment, the second adds a new circumstance of also despising the judgment of men.

In Divine Scripture, this shamelessness and recklessness are greatly emphasized, and the prophet Isaiah addresses it in his third chapter, highlighting the wickedness of the children of Israel: "The look on their faces testifies against them," and it reveals who they are. Their shamelessness is so great that in their expressions, you can see their contempt for virtue and their satisfaction in their wickedness. "They parade their sin like Sodom; they do not hide it." Rebuking His people through the mouth of Jeremiah (Jeremiah 3), the LORD says: "You have the brazen look of a prostitute; you refuse to blush with shame." Here, Jeremiah gives reason for you to consider the shamelessness of the world and how we have jointly provoked God's wrath against us.

In what Republic of Gentiles would what is favored in ours be tolerated, that there are, in the public streets and squares and around the sacred temples, public houses of dishonesty, and public persons who, with all their displays, with all the effort and diligence they can muster, make known the profession by which they live? They are so content and take such pride in it that they stay awake at night to publicize who they are to the young and the old, to the foolish and the wise, and to everyone, whether they want to know or not. And there is such permissiveness in these things or in things similar to these, that at every step, in towns with the name of Christians, even in temples and divine offices, there are outfits, talks, and interactions that suggest nothing but blatant vanity without any shame from those who understand it, rather encouraging and enjoying that it is understood and seen.

What else, let us see, is standing in the path of sinners? Standing in this path is everyone who leads a scandalous life; who, through bad company, bad behavior, or conversation, causes judgments and scandals in the hearts and mouths of their neighbors; and there is no excuse, for they place themselves and stand in a path where they will be judged by all, causing them to be regarded as so disdainful of those who see or judge them that they care nothing about being in that path. It would be a lengthy account to list all those who are implicated in standing in the path of sinners, for it includes all those who are so overcome by their passions and interests that they disdain being seen and found in such a path.

The avaricious ones in the first condition acquire by tricks and deceit, negotiating beneath the surface; those in the second condition are publicly usurers and robbers. The first tyrants were cautious; the second are shameless. The murderers of the first condition killed in their hearts and through secret plots and paths; these others boast publicly of their revenges. The adulterers of the first were clandestine and solitary; those of the second are public scandals of their wicked lives. Blessed is the one who is neither of the first nor of the second; who neither finds himself in the counsel nor follows the opinion of the wicked, nor is ever found in the public path of sinners.

We have spoken of the first two conditions briefly enough for what could be said and needed to be said, though too long for the time and patience of the listeners. Now it remains for us to speak of the third, which is: not to sit in the seat of pestilence. The interpreter here has wisely conveyed more the force of the sentence than the rigor of the word. In the original Hebrew, it is "seat of scoffers"; the interpreter rendered it as "chair of pestilence," and with very good reason, for no pestilence can equal the hearts of the sinners mentioned here, and the harm they do to the world. Not only did the Seventy translate it this way, signifying by this term "pestilence" the vice and wickedness of the scoffers, but we also find that St. Jerome did the same in many places.

The prophet attributes sitting to this last kind of wicked, because it is typical for scoffers to gather in company with each other and take a seat in places where they can observe and judge the lives and works of their brothers, making everything a subject of mockery and derision, spending their time on this and considering it their principal contentment and happiness. As the prophet says elsewhere (Psalm 69) in the name of Christ our Redeemer: "Those who sit at the gate speak against me," meaning a public and exposed place, "and I am the song of the drunkards." Here we see who exactly these people are that the Psalm mentions, the idle folk of very wicked idleness, who have no other aim in this world but to seek pleasure, in whatever way they can achieve it, even if it is at great cost and great harm to all others. There is no need for many examples; the world is full of such vagabonds, though many of them do not seem like vagabonds.

Just as it is said of envy that it thrives on others' misfortunes and is thus satisfied and content, so our scoffers make it their main activity to envy and scrutinize the goods and lives of their neighbors, interpreting everything and making it all a matter of mockery and derision, deriving great satisfaction and pleasure from it. Many of them, after passing through the first two types of wickedness mentioned above, end up in this third category, and if there are any among them who do not engage in their actions, at least none are without their mindset and disposition. Whoever mocks and derides the good and bad of his companion is ready to do him any other harm if given the occasion and opportunity. You should not lightly consider these sinners and their deeds because you will see that their number is greater than you think; their sin is greater than what either I or you can exaggerate, and the misery of our life is such that it is regarded as a kind of entertainment and pastime and the most followed exercise that the world has.

The others, the wicked and the sinners, seem to pursue some interests and ends in their deeds, although as bad as they are; but these others are such that, even if it only increases their pastime, they receive great pleasure from inventing or witnessing the misfortunes of others. Their counsels and laughter are the things that make others weep. They mock others' poverty, and they mock wealth; they mock disgrace, and they mock honor; they mock sadness, and they mock joy; they mock death, and they mock life; they mock vice, and they mock virtue. If it were left to their choice, they would rather see evil and misfortune in others' houses than virtue and happiness; but when they cannot have more, they treat everything the same way—prosperity and adversity, good and not so good: they interpret everything to one end.

You can well believe that those with such habits will have such mockery and such venom in their hearts, and you will see it in action, that to twist everything into their mockery and derision, they always add or remove, and their conversations are rarely without lies and false testimony. It is insufficient to discuss men. They also mock sacred things and mock God himself.

One of the main parts of their wit is this; nor can anything else be expected from one who finds so much pleasure and delight in sin just because it is sin. Solomon describes them, which is not from my mind, saying (Proverbs 2) that their malice is such that "doing wrong, they rejoice in the perversities of vice." And elsewhere, he says that the fool of this madness, which truly is madness from the hand of the devil, considers sin a jest and a matter of mockery (Proverbs 14), and "to do abomination is like laughter to the fool" (Proverbs 10).

This is the idleness that the world most values, which, as the teacher of many evils, according to *Ecclesiasticus* (33), ultimately teaches this to its disciples. They are so content and satisfied with their good office; so without fear and reverence of God; so without shame and law of men, that they are almost abandoned by divine doctrine, and in a certain way, they are forsaken, and as men from whom health and remedy can be expected with great difficulty, it is said that even to advise them, one should not deal with them. The wise man says in Proverbs (9): "He who corrects a scoffer brings shame upon himself, and he who rebukes a wicked man incurs injury."

From great roots of wickedness, it is necessary that great and abundant fruits of evil grow, as we mostly see in these scoffers, who are often the mature branches of the roots of the first two types we have discussed: the wicked and the sinners. The parents who engage in the first two practices usually raise children who engage in the latter. For this purpose, they accumulate estates and build houses so that their offspring may have the space to sit in the seat of scoffers and from there mock everything God does and what the devil does. Not only do the rich engage in this, but they also have as disciples many poor people who, instead of working, sustain themselves by being vagabonds, gathering rumors and news, and collecting fuel to add to the fire of others' derision.

I want to conclude with this, noting only two things for a complete understanding of the verse. The first is that through these three types of sins, in the order and words in which they are presented, we are shown how men ultimately become abominable and wicked. First, it says to walk, then to stand or stop, and finally to sit. First, it mentioned counsel, then path; finally, it mentions the seat and sitting. This is the order and rule by which sinners ascend and grow in their wickedness. Initially, they harbor malice in their hearts; they use it as counsel, treating it as secretly as possible, negotiating in darkness, and striving with all their might to maintain a facade of hypocrisy to excuse and justify themselves before men. But when this cannot fulfill or satisfy their interests, many break free from this pretense and, disregarding all shame, resolve to achieve their desires, regardless of what others think, provided they have secure power and tyranny to do as they wish. The third stage they reach is to discard all law of humanity and the natural inclination with which we are all born, not only failing to empathize with the miseries and troubles of others but finding pleasure in them and adding to them with their jests, malice, and cunning.

They mock the lineage and low fortune of others; they mock poverty, the persecution and toil of the poor, the fidelity of the loyal, the clarity of the truthful, the modest ambition of those who are neither greedy nor meddling, the almsgiving of the merciful, the religion of the Christian, the virtue and those who follow it, the devotion of the pious, the prayer of the devout. Finally, there is nothing good or bad, just or unjust, happy or unhappy, that is not a subject of mockery in this circle of scoffers.

They are placed last in the verse as the most perverse and wicked type of sinners, because, if you look closely, their main profession is to mock Divine Providence; their pride is of the same kind as Lucifer's and worse if that were possible. They mock the states in which God has placed each one; what His justice and mercy allow; the cross He places on the righteous; the poverty and paths through which He calls many to repentance; the gifts He distributes to men. They attribute to themselves and want to persuade others that they are elevated and superior to all; that they are not of that lowliness or that fortune; not subject to those circumstances, not to that poverty and injuries; that ignorance cannot touch them, nor any kind of disaster, and, as if secure that such things could never happen to them as to others, they laugh at God's judgment and live in the world without any sign of fearing it.

All these, who are more numerous than you might think, and let each put his hand on his heart and see if he is one of them, are not only not Christians but also deviate from the condition and nature of men. They are lawless and heartless, and not only do they fail to recognize that they are like other men; not only do they not help with the labors and needs of other men, as human law demands; but they make themselves idols on earth; they want to be new gods, exempt and secure from adversity in their own eyes. They mock human labors; derive their pleasures and blessedness from them; add to them with their deeds; magnify them with their lies; calumniate them with their cunning; elevate them with their testimonies; and seated in their chairs, gathered in their conversations, without weapons in hand, without being the murderers judged by the world, they exercise the most savage form of cruelty on all humanity, which no wild beast is capable of exercising. For the wild beast would only take life, and in this would end its ferocity; these take away honor; take away religion; take away truth; increase the tears and sorrows of the afflicted with their mockery, and do not spare the dead, so that when they speak of them as they do the living, they resurrect some to hurt others.

The first type we mentioned, the wicked, experienced some torment in hiding (as much as they could) the malice in their hearts; they engaged in wicked counsels. The second type, sinners, although not as burdened, were still subject to significant matters and were in the middle of the path, inviting with their bad example and their persistence in evil. Those who walked had labor, and those who stood still had labor. But these last ones have seats in which they sit. Their wickedness is their pleasure, and without it, they would lose all their recreation. They are lawless and inhumane: not only do they blaspheme against God, but against nature as well; whatever can be judged about them, they dismiss and leave behind, just to enjoy the sweetness of their mockery. Blessed is the man who did not sit in the seat of these, nor was in their company, nor had their disposition.

The other thing I said you should understand is that by these three actions we have named, all the actions of man are understood, because, if you look closely, every man ordinarily either walks, stands still, or sits. Therefore, we must understand that the Prophet teaches us here that the man will be blessed who has none of his actions be evil, nor has participation or company with the wicked; who has no malice in his heart, nor example in bad deeds, nor contentment in sin, nor disdain for Divine Providence, nor for the judgment of men, nor for the judgment of God—which is the ultimate to which man's malice rises, as we have seen in the last kind of wicked, those who sit in the seat of mockery, derision, and blasphemy. And since we have discussed the blessedness of the flesh, and advised man to depart from it as from great unhappiness and misery, it is just that we continue with the true blessedness that God wishes for His own. Comparing one with the other, the ugliness of what seems so good in the eyes of foolish men will be more clearly seen, as well as the beauty and greatness of what the Divine Word has promised and assured to those who follow His counsel. Let us see how deceitful and perishable is the glory and pomp of the world; how certain and unending is the glory that the Lord has prepared for those who serve Him.

The Second Sermon

Antes es su voluntad empleada en la ley del Señor, y en la ley de El pensara de día y de noche.[9]

THE PROPHET taught us in the first verse of the Psalm what a man must avoid to be blessed; in this second verse, he teaches what he must follow and put into practice for the complete and true fulfillment of his blessedness. It is not enough for a man to turn away from evil; he must also do good so that God may be served by him and count him among His own. Man was not created to be idle; he must have activity in this life, suitable to a creature and to a work made by the hand of the Lord. "Cease to do evil; learn to do good," says the prophet Isaiah (1). The reason why the avoidance of evil was mentioned first, before the good that must be done, we already explained in the first verse: it follows that, as we discussed the one, we now discuss the other.

He says that the blessed man has his will employed in the law of the Lord and meditates on it day and night. The source of blessedness is God, and for this reason, everything that leads us to Him can in some way be called blessedness, and thus it is called in Divine Scripture. The thing that draws us closest to Him, that gives us the certain assurance that we will always be with Him and in possession of His goods, is the keeping of His law. By law, we understand here not the religion each one invents, nor things without spirit and without light from

---

9. "but his delight is in the law of the Lord, and on his law he meditates day and night" (Ps. 1:2, ESV).

heaven, but the commandments that God has given to man and wants to be written in his heart, and with His favor and help, to be executed and put into practice without hypocrisy and duplicity. Man has no greater treasure in the world than the law of the Lord, for as the most beautiful, most just, and most holy thing is His divine will, the greatest gift that comes from His merciful hand is that He gives us a certain guide and rule to know and understand it.

The greatest reflection and representation, the thing that gives us the most certain signs of who God is, are His commandments and law. Just as He is most beautiful, pure, and free from all blemish, full of goodness and power, justice and mercy, so His law is a rule of purity and a mirror of beauty; a path of goodness, justice, and mercy; weapons that make the keeper greatly powerful and lead him to victory over all the dangers and adversities of the world. The most certain sign of following a path of blessedness and already being blessed is having a great desire to know the law that the Lord demands of him and how He wishes to be served by him and in what things he must engage.

The most verified rule of being led astray is to avoid the true knowledge of what God asks, to seek and desire ignorance, and not to want to attain full knowledge of such guidance, thus walking falsely and deceitfully. By this path of desire and keeping the law of heaven, we know all the saints walked, because whoever is certain that only one path leads to blessedness will undoubtedly desire to know it fully, with all the particulars and guidance he can attain if he truly seeks to reach such an end. "Teach me, O LORD, the way of your statutes, and I will keep it to the end. Give me understanding, and I will keep your law and observe it with my whole heart" (Psalm 119).

David wisely contrasts these two things: (i) what the wicked, sinners, and scoffers follow, with (ii) the commandments and law of the Lord. Just as the former leads to the misfortune and destruction of men, the latter brings true happiness; and just as the former originates from the malice of the human heart and is its own natural fruit, the latter proceeds from divine guidance and mercy. Just as the deeds of the wicked insult God's goodness and justice, the deeds in accordance with the law honor and serve Him, providing clear signs of who the Lord and Master is who created man. The wicked have secret malice and evil counsel in their hearts, public works on their path, and mockery and derision in their seats; likewise, those who follow God's law have purity in their souls, holy exemplary works in their hands, and pious company and conversation with others. By the first three actions—walking, standing, and sitting—we understand all human actions; so, when we say here that one should meditate on the law of the Lord day and night, we mean that all the works of those who wish to be blessed must be derived from and conformed to God's law.

The first requirement here is that a man's will be engaged in the law of the Lord. It is in vain for one to think he will be blessed by employing his wealth, hands, eyes, or any other thing in exercises and works that claim to serve God if he has not first offered and dedicated his will to His law. All the evil and multitude of evils discussed in the first verse, we said, have their source in the human heart. The fruit of the wickedness is in walking in evil counsel; its fruit is standing in the path of sinners; what arises from there is envy, mockery, and lack of piety toward neighbors. "What comes out of the heart," says our Redeemer, "is what defiles a person" (Matthew 15). Thus, we proceed here and say that the entire foundation of blessedness is having the law of the Lord in one's heart, because if it is there, we are assured there will be no evil counsel, no evil path, no evil seat; rather, there will necessarily be the opposite—holy counsel, holy path, and holy seat.

The Law of God is the principal enemy of those three evil things; they cannot coexist in a single heart. When the Law arrives, it immediately banishes and expels all those things: it is like a knife that cuts and a fire that consumes. The Law of the Lord, as our Prophet says elsewhere, is an unblemished law that converts and comforts the simple. The commandments of the LORD are right, rejoicing the heart; the commandment of the LORD is pure, enlightening the eyes (Psalm 19). It is clear, then, that the Law of God, and all those things we mentioned that the wicked practice, will not make good company in the heart of man.

Now, we must discuss what it means to have one's will set on the Law of the Lord. This we shall explain briefly, and then we will proceed to the fruits and the blessedness that result from it. To have one's will engaged in the Law of the Lord is nothing other than to have a great desire to enact what the Law commands and to take great delight in doing so. A person must find these signs in their heart to know they are on the path to blessedness. Anyone who follows other routes, whatever they may be, and convinces themselves that they will achieve certain blessedness that way is deceived and lost. This is the sentiment that the saints had. This is the sentiment that Christians must have, and this is the point they must strive to reach. Meanwhile, as long as they are far from this, they should know they are far from God.

The judgments of the LORD, says the Prophet, are true and altogether righteous: more desirable than gold, even much fine gold, and sweeter than honey and the honeycomb (Psalm 19). First, we assert that it is greatly desirable to enact the commandments of God. This desire arises from the knowledge of the justice and beauty of the divine will when man, aided by heavenly favor, truly understands that such a holy and just will can only issue commandments that are supremely just and holy; that such a generous and boundless will can demand nothing of man that is not for his great and incomparable treasure; cannot impart any counsel that is not of great mercy and profound wisdom; cannot show us a path that is not of great security; cannot give us advice that is not most faithful and on which we can be sure and certain that it will never fail us: finally, that we cannot aspire to greater dignity, nor perform a more illustrious and significant act, nor achieve greater honor or greatness, nor find greater contentment, than to be so closely aligned with God that we desire the same things as Him; that, despite the Creator being so far above us creatures, we can achieve such great participation in His supreme goodness that we appear to align with Him in judgment and will. You, Lord, say that this is good, and we say the same; you say you desire it, and we also desire it.

When a man has considered all this, and the light of divine favor has awakened and enlightened him to recognize it, a great desire to fulfill the commandments of God is kindled in his heart. And from this same desire, when he enacts them, springs a great contentment. "I have loved your commandments," says David, "more than gold, even more than fine gold" (Psalm 119). For each time a man puts into effect what God commands, he must think and consider what we have just said and can and should say in his heart: "Help me, Lord, to carry this out, for I am certain that by this path I will see You; that this is a way without danger and without betrayal: by any other, I would be lost, and by this alone am I free; I follow counsel with which it is impossible to be deceived; I have a promise that will never fail; I travel with company that ensures my safety; Your wisdom accompanies me to guide me; Your power to defend me; and though there be many enemies and dangers, I have nothing to fear."

You, Lord, are an enemy to all evil, but you consider me a friend. In this task to which I now set my hands, you have your eyes fixed. Your attention is awakened to it, as it is something that pleases and serves you. What more could I desire or ask than to want what you want? In brief words, we have explained what it means for a man to have his will aligned with the law of the Lord, though it is a long journey to achieve it. It requires much effort and perseverance, and it cannot be attained without God's intervention, which is readily available to aid us if we invoke it with an awareness of our weakness and with true faith.

Let us now proceed to the differences between the blessedness of the wicked and that of the righteous, so we can better understand how false and deceptive the former is, and how certain and true the latter. The first, which we have already discussed, is the blessedness of the flesh and of men subject to the law and tyranny of sin; the second is that of the spirit and of those who have been freed by the blood of Jesus Christ, and through this freedom, have gained the strength and power to fulfill the law of the Lord.

The carnal man seeks and derives his sense of blessedness from those three primary things: walking in the counsel of the wicked, standing in the way of sinners, and sitting in the seat of mockers. In this, he finds what he desires. The greedy man is restless, seeing that another is wealthier than he is, and tormented by that envy, he seeks similar counsel to acquire more wealth or at least to match that of his neighbor. The ambitious man follows this path, seeking counsel and companionship, favors and conspiracies, cunning and strategies to fulfill his desires. The same goes for the deceitful, the murderer, and the vindictive.

The one who is openly wicked and whose appetites and bad inclinations are so unrestrained that they leave no room for moderation, consoles and excuses his evil by observing that many others follow the same path, and not only are they tolerated, but they are also favored by the world. The mockers, who ridicule the good and the bad they see in others and in their neighbors' households, as men without God's law and without human reason and inclination, place their blessedness not in the goods they attain but in the misfortunes of others and the pleasure they derive from them. To enjoy this twisted sense of blessedness, they seek a place of rest, companions who will assist them, idleness that will guide them to savor their pleasure; they take delight in scrutinizing, exaggerating, slandering, and raising false accusations that bring them contentment while causing annoyance and harm to their neighbor. In these things we have summed up where the foolish flesh of the miserable men of the world places its blessedness, and through these paths it seeks it: through the counsel and cunning of the wicked, the way of sinners, and the seat and company of scoffers.

The blessedness of the spirit, which God desires for His followers in this world as a pledge and assurance of the blessedness they will have in the next, consists in the counsel of the righteous, in the way and example of the just, and in the diligence and exercise of charity. All of this is found and derived from the word and law of the Lord. Therefore, our verse says that the man who will be truly blessed is the one who has his heart inclined to this law and who meditates on it day and night. For such a person not only avoids and distances himself from the evil counsel, way, and seat of the wicked but also seeks new counsel, a new path, and an exercise in which to engage and employ himself.

This counsel is found in the law of the Lord, which He gave to His servant Abraham so that through it, he might be blessed. "I am the Almighty God; walk before me and be perfect" (Genesis 17). This is the true counsel, given by a good friend, which is from the Lord Himself who created man and in whose hands and will it is to make him blessed; for this purpose, He created him. And since He says that the true way to become blessed is to please His eyes and follow His will, we can safely take such advice and, if we choose to follow it, can consider our blessedness certain from here on.

This counsel was further elaborated by divine mercy in the two tablets of the law, which Moses received, written by the finger of God, to preach and teach to His people. On them are written the Ten Commandments, which are nothing but a more abundant and comprehensive explanation of what the Lord had commanded Abraham when He told him to be perfect and walk before Him, pleasing and serving Him. As the blindness of man continued to advance daily, and through his bad habits and examples took deeper root, divine mercy provided a clearer and more detailed light of His commandments and law. Thus, Scripture says that the two tablets of the testimony were written by the finger of God (Exodus 31), signifying that they came from His hand and were marked and signed by His name; in this, He warns everyone that what is written there is His law, the way He desires to be served, and that in it lies their perfection, goodness, and blessedness.

From this, you can see how much better the counsel is for those who follow the path of these commandments compared to the others, whom we previously discussed as following the counsel of the wicked. God reveals His will to man out of love and with the desire that man puts it into action and becomes blessed. "The word of the LORD is right," says Psalm 33, "and all His works are done in truth. He loves righteousness and justice; the earth is full of the goodness of the LORD." Everything He commands and ordains; everything He counsels; everything with which He advises men is firm, certain, and most faithful. There is nothing in it that is not from a true Lord and a true friend; His word cannot deceive, nor can His truth fail. The earth is full of His mercy, meaning that in the matter of such importance to man, which is to know what the will of God is, how He desires to be served, He has made it known and confirmed it with His own hand. He is a source of infinite mercy; in no way can He better manifest who He is or act according to His nature than by advising men of His will, the path they should follow to reach Him, and the true knowledge of His commandments and law.

We have spoken about the counsel that the blessed find in the law of the Lord, and it is fitting now to discuss the path found within it, so that one may stand firm and persevere on it.

You have heard of the path of sinners where many stand, which is the public bad example and public bad life set out like a road and marketplace for the judgment and provocation of others. We declared that those whose attachment to their wickedness is so strong that, when they can do no more, disregarding all fear and shame of men, they make a public and manifest display of their thoughts and deeds. Likewise, the one who takes the counsel of the Lord, if they truly take it, has their will so firmly and affectionately set on it that they are not content nor can they bear to keep it in their heart or for themselves alone as a secret counsel; instead, they publicly display it and manifest it with deeds. Whenever necessary, they make a path and a public proclamation of God's commandments, persevering and remaining constant in them, imitating those who followed that path and inviting and provoking others with their example to follow it as well.

The principal purpose for which man is placed on earth by the hand of God is to be a reflection and representation of Him. In their actions and deeds, man should testify of their Creator, and after fulfilling this duty, they should be taken and placed in a position where they have perpetual imitation with Him in immortality, glory, dominion, and blessedness. Men have strayed and deviated so far from the purpose for which they were created that by the account and testimony of their actions, they seem more to represent the serpent that deceived them than the Master and Lord who made them. The more widespread this deviation is and the greater the infamy that, in the judgment of men, results for the Lord who initially formed them and gave them being, the more the righteous must put in greater diligence and strive with all their strength to give a true and holy testimony in their works of their Maker and Lord. This is the path in which they must stand; this is the example they must set for others; this must be their perseverance and steadfastness.

Indeed, the multitude of sinners is so great, the path they tread so wide, and the shamelessness and determination with which they stand upon it so overwhelming, that it will be very arduous for anyone who wishes to take another path and maintain constancy and firmness on it. Great strength and effort are required so that the force and multitude of the others do not overthrow and carry him away. The Redeemer of the world says that the path to heaven is narrow and that few travel it; the gate is narrow, and few enter through it, and it is necessary to strive and struggle not to be left outside.

As we warn man about one thing, we also warn him about the other: just as God teaches man the path to blessedness, He also reveals the inconveniences and labors he will encounter on it and how he should deal with them if he wishes to reach the end. One of the greatest difficulties, and you may well say it is the greatest and most principal of all that confront those who want to follow the path of truth and maintain firmness and perseverance in it, is the violence and multitude of those who take the opposite path. It is a strong challenge for human weakness to see that the path of his neighbors is wide and smooth, while his is narrow and uphill; to see that the other is restful and his is laborious; that the others have gain and pleasure, while he has loss and sorrow; that the others have honor and he has affronts; that the others have company and he has solitude. This is a very grave temptation, which not only overthrows and leads astray the common crowd of weak-minded and simple people but also disrupts many men of good intentions who had achieved greater insight and constancy and had begun to walk with some determination on the path of righteousness. The tyranny and power of the multitude in all things is great, and most things are governed and ruled by it; but where it causes the greatest harm and destruction is in matters concerning the path of God's law. This tyranny canonizes and de-canonizes whatever it pleases and whatever its mad judgment determines.

It destroys and discredits good and ancient customs, just and holy laws, and introduces and approves bad ones. It acts and undoes in religion and every kind of virtue as it fancies; it banishes God's law from the world, strips it of the title of justice, and bestows it on the law of the devil and whatever else it pleases. It reigns not only through bad example, bad customs, and deeds but also through violent oppression. The former alone would be sufficient to cause great harm in human misery and frailty without the latter, but combined, you can see what evil results, and we experience it every day. Man desires company by his nature; his vanity craves applause; his madness demands esteem and the publicizing of his deeds; the favor of those who see and hear them; the approval and acclaim of the world.

Therefore, consider, for my sake, on one side, the path and marketplace of the world so leveled and approved by its customs and laws; so widened by the multitude; so frequented and well-trodden by those who walk it; so favored by its own voices and clamor; so privileged and exempt from the very exceptions it has claimed for itself; so stocked with the pomp, follies, and delights of its appetites, and consider on the other a narrow path of its own making, uphill by the nature of the way; solitary because it is not frequented; desolate due to its solitude; filled with thorns from little use; devoid of resting places; subject to dangers and robberies; prepared for inconveniences and discomforts. Now imagine a man attempting to enter this path in the presence of the other world that walks the other way, and that he himself sees he is alone; if he lifts his eyes to the path, he finds it harsh; if he turns them to his appetite, he finds it inclined to the smoothness and things of the other; if he considers the example, he sees all company far away; and above all this, the others jeer at him, calling him a fool; they mock his folly; they entice him with the comforts and the broadness of their plazas; the misery of the path he takes; they tempt him in a thousand ways, waking and stirring him in a thousand manners. Believe me, it will be a great thing if this little man does not turn back, and despite the jeers and scorn the world heaps upon him, continues forward through his labors and the narrowness and dangers of his path.

Much has been said, yet it is the least of what there is. The treacherous world is not content with following its path and letting the poor soul follow his own; rather, it pursues him with great anger, and with tyrannical hands, it draws him in, tramples on him, and mistreats him. It perpetrates countless injustices upon him, depriving him of life in a thousand ways, because it cannot tolerate anyone departing from its revelry, straying from its path, refusing to serve and obey its vanity, pursuing a virtue it does not follow, or approving and holding in high regard what its customs have already discredited and devalued.

Despite all this, we say that the man who wishes to be blessed must not only turn away from the counsel of the wicked; he must not only have the counsel of God's law in his heart; but he must also set himself on the path, stand firm, and persevere on it. He must climb the slopes, and if he finds himself alone, he must remain alone; he must fight with himself and with all others; resist their onslaught; endure hunger amid their ill-gotten abundance; affirm the truth even if all others deny it; be willing to lose his life on that path rather than turn back. For he ascends while others descend; he travels the road to blessedness while others head toward misfortune; he seeks the level ground while others seek the precipice. The hardships of his narrow path last very little, but the rest at the inn has no end;

the pleasures and contentment that others are gorged on will end in a few days, but the torments of their misfortune will have no end nor reduction as long as God is God.

It may seem that I have placed the blessed man in great solitude, leading him through a very narrow and barren path. However, this is not a notion I have concocted, nor a situation exaggerated by my words; let the experience of what transpires speak for itself. And since you rarely see in these matters what is right before your eyes, and never realize the certainty of your perdition until you are beyond remedy, let the Lord of the law and counsel of which we speak, the Giver and Confirmer of the blessedness we promise, affirm it.

If you recall, we mentioned that God spoke to Abraham, teaching him the way He wanted to be served and how to be blessed, saying: "Walk before me and be perfect." The moment He placed this law and counsel in Abraham's heart, He immediately set him on his path: "Leave your country, Abraham, leave your relatives and your father's house and go to the land that I will show you; there I will multiply your offspring." Here you see the solitude of God's chosen one, taken out of his natural environment; exiled from his relatives and acquaintances; brought to the land of Canaan, populated by enemies of God, by idolatrous people, infamous and contaminated by all the evils of the world. This solitude alone would be enough to make the path very harsh, and on top of all this, God wanted to narrow it further by testing him with hunger; with new and sudden exiles; with many and various kinds of persecutions.

I could extend this discussion by bringing many examples to support this point, but time does not permit, and the example I will now mention will suffice to confirm everything said. The Redeemer of life, who regained for men the lost blessedness and who taught the way to it with His very word, was not content with the example of His own person; He also warned His disciples about the labor and narrowness and the great solitude of the path they were to follow. What greater solitude can be imagined in the world than to separate men in such a way, to estrange them so completely from others, that the world itself does not recognize them as its own nor treats them as such?

"You," He says (John 15), "though you are in the world, are not of the world; I have alienated you from it. My doctrine and my truth have made you alone; you are strangers and foreigners. Therefore, do not be surprised if the world treats you as strangers, for you are not of the world, and it treats you like a stepmother, for you are children of another mother. The favor and approval you will find in it will be that you are accused as deceivers, and the world will think that it is serving God by taking your life." If this warning proved true, let St. Paul bear witness as one of them, and describe how the world treated them. "We have become," he says, "like the scum of the world, the refuse of all things" (1 Corinthians 4).

And to see the blindness and madness of this miserable world, it does all this and does not understand that it is doing it, and swears that it is not doing it. It commits the very crime and insists that it is praying; you catch it red-handed with theft, and it believes it is giving you its property; it is cutting off your head, and it says it is healing your wounds. See how blind and wicked it is; and so blind. The cause of this, we have mentioned; I do not know if you understood. It is a friend of the wide path, of the well-trodden way, of the law and approval of many; it always follows the crowd and avoids solitude; and being mad, it believes that God shares its same condition, that He is as fond of the many and holds the few in little regard.

To the world, it seems impossible and illogical that God's satisfaction and delight could rest in a few solitary, despised individuals, to whom He has denied so much of the things He created, and that He would wish His blessedness and heaven for so few, while so much of the world, to whom He has shown so many mercies and in whom His works so greatly shine, would be left aside. It seems to the world that heaven and blessedness are designed for the many and the great, not for the few and the small. How could such a great and powerful Lord, who created the world for His service, be satisfied with so few and discontented with so many?

Let me illustrate this with an example. We read in the book of Job (1) that Satan appeared before God and was asked where he had come from. He responded, "From roaming throughout the earth, going back and forth on it." God then asked, "Have you considered my servant Job? There is no one on earth like him; he is blameless and upright, a man who fears God and shuns evil." Despite Satan conquering many hosts and claiming much of the earth as his own, God put forth Job as His own, a just man. See here how the Lord is content with the few if the many refuse to be His. The reason for this can be discussed later, as time is short, but someday I will prove with God's help how this makes much sense, if not according to human laws, then at least according to God's laws.

Now, we must discuss the third aspect found in the law of the Lord, which corresponds to the seat of scoffers. We have already addressed what corresponds to the first two aspects, which are the counsel of the wicked and the path of sinners. Just as we find good and holy counsel in God's law to counter bad counsel; a good and holy path and example to counter the path of sinners, so we find a good exercise against the bad seat and ill rest of mockery and scorn. This exercise is charity, which not only does not delight in the misfortunes and shames of others but also covers all faults and a multitude of sins (Proverbs 10; 1 Peter 4). Charity is a cloak and a cover for the defects of one's neighbor. It is said to cover a multitude of sins because there is no one for whom it does not feel compassion; no one whom it does not at least wish to conceal and excuse, so that while one's neighbor may be judged by God, they are not judged by men.

How contrary this diligence is to the restless idleness of those who sit in the seat of mockery and scorn. Such individuals not only expose and publicize sins but also mock virtues; not just faults, but natural defects and even the works of God, mocking what their neighbor cannot help. This mockery goes even further. Where there is little fault, it magnifies it; where it is minor, it exaggerates it; where there is none, it invents it; where there is good, it wants it judged as bad and to appear as such. In the law of God, there is only charity toward friends and enemies, charity toward sin and sinner alike. "He who loves his neighbor has fulfilled the law" (Romans 13).

How contrary to the mocker and scorner are the precepts of the law of God! Let it testify for itself when it expressly commands: "Do not curse the deaf or put a stumbling block in front of the blind, but fear your God. Rise in the presence of the aged, show respect for the elderly and revere your God. I am the Lord" (Leviticus 19). You should not lightly pass over the importance of this law and its charity, for it shows respect for the frailty of the elderly, whom everyone mocks, and here commands that they be honored by all. Consideration is also shown for the deaf, who cannot hear or respond, and for the blind, who cannot see. From these particular cases, you can derive a general rule for the importance and practice of charity against the third kind of sinners who take pleasure in the seat of scoffers.

We have thus completed the discussion of man's blessedness, explaining how he can find remedy in the law of God for all the obstacles that may hinder him from being blessed. Let us now proceed further, continuing our explanation, so that you may more easily understand and know how to find the remedy to put it into practice. Our verse says that the blessed man has his will in the law of the Lord and meditates on it day and night. This meditation not only means the exercise of thought but also the execution and work of hands. It would be vain contemplation to merely spend time considering the law of God and its marvels and remain content with this without applying diligence to works. Consideration serves to inform about the law and what it commands or prohibits, and this is directed toward action, which, if lacking, renders the initial effort in vain. We will discuss this further shortly.

Now, let us explain what it means: "day and night." This is to be understood in the same way as the Apostle teaches when he says to pray without ceasing (1 Thessalonians 5; Luke 18), which means to turn to the law of God in all our needs and for all our actions; to take instruction and guidance from it, considering it as a general rule for our entire life, for our words and deeds. Just as we said in the first verse that walking, standing, and sitting encompassed all of man's actions, we now say that day and night signify the same.

Previously, we understood this to mean turning away from all evil deeds; here, we understand it to mean following what is good, so that in all things, one first seeks counsel from the law of God and acts according to its commands. One should accept adversity with patience, forgive injury with the forgiveness and endurance the law mandates, embrace prosperity with temperance, and with the moderation it requires. Finally, remember that it is written (Deuteronomy 4 and 12) that none who enter into God's obedience should act according to their own judgment and opinion, but according to what the law commands; consider their judgment vain, their opinion false and lost; renounce their wisdom, and be, in this, an enemy to themselves, judging and esteeming themselves on earth as blind and without guidance, having no other light or guide but the Word of God.

"Your word is a lamp for my feet, a light on my path," says the Prophet (Psalm 119). The wicked followed and gave bad counsel, and by it, they performed their works and walked in their ways. The just, to be blessed, should take for themselves the counsel given by the law of God; with this, they should advise others and guide their works and those of others. "These words that I command you today shall be on your heart, and you shall teach them diligently to your children, and you shall talk of them when you sit in your house, and when you walk by the way, and when you lie down, and when you rise. You shall bind them as a sign on your hand, and they shall be as frontlets between your eyes. You shall write them on the doorposts of your house and on your gates" (Deuteronomy 6). This is how the meditation on God's law is to be done, day and night.

The inclination of our heart is continually towards evil (Genesis 6). It has bad counsel and bad inclinations from the days of youth (Genesis 8), which is the time of its transgression. It is necessary, therefore, that for such bad and ordinary counsel, we also have an ordinary remedy, always advising ourselves with this holy, pure, and unsuspicious law of certain blessedness. The devil is always waging war against us, and as the Apostle says, he prowls around like a roaring lion looking for someone to devour (1 Peter 5). We cannot resist him except with the strength of faith, and we cannot have faith except with the Word of God, employing our obedience, our heart, and our will in it.

The Prophet beautifully comprehends in this verse all the blessedness that man can attain in this life, and the certainty of the next, for it embraces all places, all the wealth of the law of the Lord. It teaches us faith, it teaches us charity, how our heart should be, what our works should be, how we should conduct ourselves with God, how we should deal with ourselves, and then with our neighbors. First, he places the law in the will, settles it in the heart, where true faith is engendered and enlivened; then he demands its exercise day and night, which, as we have already explained, means in all our actions.

All this is opposed to the three initial things mentioned in the first verse: bad counsel, evil deeds, and the seat of scoffers, from which it clearly follows that the entire doctrine of the second verse, which we are currently discussing, is clear. Works that do not come from the heart are false and treacherous. The heart that does not produce works is lukewarm and false. Faith and charity are neither partial nor self-interested; they do not stop with those who possess them; they desire to serve everyone. Faith and love are sacrifices to God; they purify the heart for itself, enlarge it, and make it generous toward one's neighbor. This is the final test, and if there is a lack here, it is a sure sign that everything else was false, and no matter how rich one may be, it will be unprofitable because, if it is not beneficial to the brothers, it will not be beneficial to the one who possesses it.

"If I speak in the tongues of men and of angels but do not have charity, I am only a resounding gong or a clanging cymbal. If I have the gift of prophecy and can fathom all mysteries and all knowledge, and if I have a faith that can move mountains, but do not have charity, I am nothing. If I give all I possess to the poor and give over my body to hardship that I may boast, but do not have charity, I gain nothing" (1 Corinthians 13). This gift is essential for men to be blessed.

Everything we have discussed is fundamentally opposed to the three things we taught that the blessed man must avoid, and it includes what must replace them. This will all be true if the root and foundation of everything are true and genuine; it will be true and genuine if the law of God is in his heart. The holy Prophet did not say, "Blessed is the man who has the law of God written," nor "the one who speaks and boasts of it," but rather, "Blessed is the man whose will is enamored with the law of the Lord," because if this is so, it is a sign that he knows it. If he knows it, this love will be so effective and powerful, he will be so pleased with what he loves, that it will necessarily bear fruit outwardly. "The law of God," says the Prophet elsewhere, "is in the heart of the righteous, and his steps do not falter" (Psalm 36). The one who has the law of God in his heart firmly and with constancy sets his feet in the works of the law of God. Whoever achieves this has achieved everything.

But who will this be? And let us praise him. This work is more difficult than anyone can imagine, and many lose themselves in it: some are overconfident, others are cowardly, because both measure themselves by their own strength. The one who trusts in himself becomes proud; when he thinks he is succeeding, he errs, and when he seems to rise, he falls. The other thought there was no power beyond his own, despaired, and fell behind. If he had known where the strength lay and how to ask for it, he would have succeeded in his endeavor and fared better by having a humble opinion of himself than the first for having an exalted one. Understand now how difficult it is, and how impossible by human strength alone, for a man to have the law of God in his heart, so that you may lose confidence in yourselves and pay attention to the second point, where we will teach you where the possibility and ease, the effort and strength, and the fulfillment of victory lie.

Man, descended from Adam, is condemned to be a servant of sin. Within his flesh and heart resides the law of the one to whom he subjected himself, which is the law of sin, whose fruit is death, displeasing to God and contrary to His justice. What benefit would it be, then, to a man who has such a law and is so subject to it, and whose flesh is so content and defeated by that law, to bring him the law of God in written form, to give him complete knowledge of it, and to declare the services required by his Creator? Indeed, it would cause him much distress and provide little benefit, as it would only serve to awaken him to his own wickedness, unsettling and saddening him by its sight, and his own wickedness would take the opportunity to trouble and weary him further.

By the law, says the Apostle Paul to the Romans (7), came the knowledge and awareness of sin; for I would not have known what coveting really was if the law had not said, "You shall not covet." What resulted from this was great disquiet for me, seeing myself subject to sin and condemned by it, because I understood that the law of God demanded righteousness and purity from that sin or condemned me for it. And my own evil desire and sin, awakened by my guilty conscience and the notification of the law, strove to resist the law that condemned it, and seemed to gain new strength against it and against me. Until then, it was as if it were asleep, and the ignorance and repose of my conscience had kept it quiet; so that it was killing me more gently and taking my life while I slept.

The law awakened my conscience; my conscience awakened my sin; it gained strength, but I did not. It raged, and it seemed to gain vigor in the justice demanded by the law, and being an enemy of it, it became its ally to condemn me; so that it is more alive and I am more dead. The conscience that was supposed to stand up for me and resist the law sided with it and became a witness against myself. I affirmed and testified that justice was required of me, that the law was holy, that the law was just, and that I was obliged to fulfill all the commandments of God. Thus, this and that have brought me to such a state that I now palpably feel the war I have always had within me, and this war has grown. For on one side I say yes, and on the other I say no. I acknowledge the law of God as holy and just, I look at my hands and my heart, and I find the opposite of what it demands and what I confess.

People who do not feel this inner conflict are soulless; they neither care about God nor themselves. They are all flesh and body, dedicating their efforts to bodily pleasure and indulgence, neglecting their soul and leaving God and fate aside. However, the wicked man who cares for his body and also wishes well for his soul, who tries to deceive God with all his cunning, aiming to please both himself and God, will feel the conflict between God's law and his conscience and sin.

Above all, this conflict is felt by those who sincerely strive to fulfill God's law with their reason and strength, for they soon realize their duplicity. When they confess to the law and their conscience that they will comply, they find their actions saying no. Some might claim that we have spoken the truth but left them without remedy, acknowledging that God's law is just and that whoever does not follow it is justly condemned. When they attempt to fulfill it and internalize it, they encounter a closed door, a great distaste for it, and a powerful inclination toward the contrary. Even if they try to deceive themselves into thinking they are obeying God's law, their conscience and their actions reveal otherwise.

This internal conflict can drive one to anger against the law, and although they may recognize its justice, they see it as harsh and wish they could appeal against it. They might feel resentment towards those who convey it, blaming them for their condemnation, although their only fault is presenting God's law plainly and truthfully, as it must be known. What has been said so far demonstrates how great and beyond human strength it is to have God's law truly in one's heart and to love it genuinely; it is vastly different from merely feigning it with words or hypocritical deeds, and trying to deceive oneself and God by claiming to follow the law.

Now, it is appropriate to discuss the remedy for all this. Let it be a general rule that all fulfillment of the law and all blessedness resulting from it presupposes the sacrifice of Jesus Christ, the true Son of God, Redeemer, and Liberator of humanity. This applies not only after the preaching and publication of the holy Gospel but also for all past time since man sinned. Just as there was always a need for special favor and strength from heaven for men to serve God and fulfill His commandments, to return to the grace and fellowship from which their sin had estranged them, so there was always a remedy available to achieve it.

This remedy was the passion of the Redeemer of the world, which is a sufficient and most just sacrifice to reconcile men with God and to obtain for them both the forgiveness of their past sins and a renewal of heart and nature, empowering them with a new disposition and vigor to serve the Lord and keep His commandments. The death of the Son of God was so pleasing to His Father that, even before it was accomplished, it produced the effects we have described in the elect. Therefore, we must consider that there were Christians not only after the Redeemer suffered but also before. They operated and served God in the same faith and favor as those who are righteous now and have always served Him.

Returning to the difficulty we found in a man's desire to be blessed, placing his will in the law of the Lord, and meditating on it day and night, we say that not only he, but also the very Prophet who wrote this and fulfilled it, was by nature a carnal man, subject to the law of sin, without the ability and strength for what he wrote. He was justified by Jesus Christ, the Justifier of men, liberated from that captivity, strengthened, and renewed with the spirit of heaven through the Son of God, in whom he placed his trust, and in his heart offered the sacrifice of his blood before the eyes of the Father.

We too must turn to this source if we wish to partake in this blessedness; here we will find forgiveness of our sins, knowledge to understand ourselves, hatred and enmity for our wicked deeds, strength and amendment for the future, eyes to behold the beauty of God, confidence to follow Him, a heart to love Him, charity towards our neighbors, and everything needed for our utmost goal of being blessed. Let our weakness not dismay us; rather, the greater it is, the more earnestly and fervently we should implore the remedy. If it is delayed, we should not despair. It is not denied to us so that we may be lost, but so that we may feel our deficiency more keenly, and feeling it, pray more earnestly and value it more highly when granted.

What was impossible for man—to be justified and to be a friend of God, impossible due to the weakness and rebellion of his flesh—is made easy by the Son of God, who, by taking on our flesh, crucified our weakness in it, and condemned our sin, so that the righteousness required by the law and the works of its commandments might be fulfilled in us (Romans 8). This teaching is not only great but so necessary for man's remedy that it is impossible to achieve it by any other means; for thus has God determined, and what He has determined in this matter is an irrevocable decree, with no appeal, no excuse, nor privilege: His word is as just and eternal.

We have often stated this, and it is necessary to repeat it many more times, because besides being deaf to this doctrine, man makes himself even more deaf, thinking he can benefit from this stubbornness, which is actually the main cause of his perdition. Since man must treat the law of God in such a way that it is firmly established and written in his heart with great love, with a will enamored of its beauty, always ready and attentive to fulfill its commands whenever they are required, and there being no shortcut or detour to escape this if he wants to be blessed, nor will it help him to exceed in outward works and displays more than all the prophets and patriarchs, it is reasonable that he learns how to attain the love of this holy law, and to put great diligence in remembering this advice and practicing it in such a way that he achieves victory.

Let the Pharisee who thought that merely outward works fulfilled the commandments of heaven be cast out; let the Muslim who places all his sanctity in certain ceremonies be cast out;

let the hypocrite who, with the name of Christian and good appearances, thinks that in God's reckoning he will be excused for the state of his heart and be pardoned because of the good appearance of his deeds be cast out. We speak here to Christians, who are required to have both a pure heart towards God, enamored with the divine law, and holy testimony of deeds, not only for the judgment of heaven but also for that of men.

Here, we have briefly recapitulated one of the main considerations discussed in the sermon, and from the many reasons that were pursued, we have summarized so that you may more easily commit it to memory and meditate on it later. I will do the same for the remaining consideration, and this should not seem burdensome to you, because in such important matters and necessary doctrines, much repetition or prolixity is required if you wish to call it that, so that those who wish to benefit can do so more easily without the multitude of reasons hindering their memory.

Recapitulating, therefore, the second consideration, I say that, in order for the first thing we have discussed—the necessity for man to embrace the law of the Lord with his heart—to be useful to the listener, it is necessary that in brief words he understands the method by which to achieve it, as it is the only and certain guarantee of blessedness. Do not think that this method is something invented by men, for it would be of little use if it were from men: it is a method taught by divine mercy, and the same Scripture that declares how the law of God should be in us also declares how we are to internalize it.

It has been discussed how inept man is for this endeavor and how he remains indifferent to the commandments of heaven even when notified that without them, he cannot reach heaven. Pay attention now, for in brief, we will teach you the method by which this can be achieved, if you desire to achieve it. Man must bring with him great vigilance, exhorting, awakening, and contending with himself for this love of the law of God. In the state he currently finds himself and in the blindness his sin has placed him, he is much more capable of judging the works of God than His law; he understands more of the beauty and order of the world than of the beauty and order of the divine law. Hence, he must continuously reflect that if the works of God are so full of beauty, wisdom, mercy, and justice, and with them, He creates, sustains, and remedies him, then His law will not be less beautiful, just, merciful, or wise, nor less a remedy for the time that remains without end, than the other works have been for this brief time we live here. Rather, he should argue that the excellence of the law is much greater than that of the works, because the latter is for a short time; the former is for being blessed as long as God exists.

This same argument is made by our Prophet (Psalm 19), deducing from the beauty and perfection of His law: "The heavens declare the glory of God; the skies proclaim the work of His hands." When a man persuades himself through this reflection of the beauty and goodness of the divine law, he must diligently strive to elevate his heart to fall in love with something so beautiful, powerful, just, and good. From these reflections, he should conceive a desire to engage so well, to please such a great Lord, to achieve this great end for which he was created.

When he finds himself reluctant to do this, with little appreciation for such greatness, with little understanding of such lofty goods, with attachments to contrary things, with inclinations towards vile, weak, and perishable things, he must understand that this is not due to a defect in the divine law or in what it commands and promises, but that this misfortune arises from himself, that his sin has placed him in such misery that he does not love his own remedy, that he is blind to such beauty, deaf to its news, foolish to consider it, mean and degraded to engage in it, and that the devil and his own sin, the world, and his own flesh are envious and treacherous and seek with all their might to prevent him from achieving such good.

From this should arise an enmity against himself and everything that opposes such a great end. He must understand that within himself he harbors another who is very treacherous, very flattering, very indulgent, and deceitful, and that by making him believe that he is himself and as much his friend as if he were himself, and that he seeks his good in all things, he is in fact his greatest enemy and seeks all his miseries and evils. Therefore, he must strive to overcome and kill this one within himself, for he is a traitor and an ally of everyone who seeks to harm him.

The weapons he must employ for this victory include all study, all diligence, and all forms of mortification. He must avenge himself on that bad companion, causing him great discomfort, bearing the cross that comes, and punishing himself rigorously because with that punishment, the traitor within him is tormented. If he encounters infamy, poverty, persecution, and hardship because of the diligence he applies, he should understand that these are the weapons with which his enemies are defeated. He should pursue victory tirelessly, for his enemies are powerful and many. He should never feel secure from them, and even when they seem dead, he should believe that they have surrounded him with greater force than before. "The one who perseveres to the end will be saved" (Matthew 10).

He must not relent in his enmity towards them and must always remember that they obstruct his love for such great beauty and seek to deprive him of such immense goods. He may say that these weapons are too burdensome for him to wield, and he speaks the truth. The Spirit of Heaven must wield them, and it is He who succeeds in conquering and killing with them; no one else can do it. We have already declared that this is achieved through Jesus Christ, our Redeemer and Lord. He will communicate with us if we can, and if we ask with an understanding of the greatness of such a gift and the necessity we have for it; if our sigh is very true, our prayer continuous, our petition anguished, and if we confess that we are in great need because of the great opposition from our enemies and from ourselves.

In this way, the eyes of the Christian begin to open to contemplate even a little of the beauty of God's law. Through this, the beginning of its sweetness and the feeling of the peace and quiet it brings is revealed. Once this is known, it is easy to understand how faithful a friend it is, how sound its counsel for both prosperity and adversity, for dealing with friends and enemies, and how certain a companion it is for never straying from the path.

Therefore, whoever, distrustful of himself and an enemy of himself because of his sin, seeks justice here and truly seeks it, should know for certain that he will find a new heart, a new will, and a desire with which to carry out what God wills.

This law will be his exercise day and night, a retreat where he can hide from the tempests of the world, where he can find secret pleasures unknown and untasted by those who do not have the commandments of heaven in their hearts, even if their house is filled with all the riches that the earth can offer. It will be a rest for his weariness, a medicine for his wounds, a comfort for his pains. Here he will find, if he wishes, guidance in

his doubts, consolation in his troubles, faith to keep him steadfast, hope to cheer him, charity to draw him closer and make
him one in spirit with the Lord he serves. And as he continues
on his path to blessedness, when the labors of this miserable life
are over, he will attain the abundance and fulfillment of a life
that lacks nothing and never ends.

The Third Sermon

Y será cono el árbol plantado a las corrientes de las aguas, que
dar su fruto a su tiempo: cuya hoja no se caerá, y todo cuanto
hiciere será prosperado.[10]

THE THINGS found in Divine Scripture, the great blessings and favors promised to men, are so exceedingly
great, so contrary to the judgment and perception of
the flesh, that, if it were only for this, there would be no one
who would not falter, partly due to lack of faith and partly due
to lack of effort. You will easily understand this if you consider
how far a mere man of the world is from the habit, knowledge, experience, and reason of all heavenly things. He is poor
and miserable; he is invited to such great wealth, and when
he measures himself, he finds himself without the vessel and
capacity for it, feeling inadequate and lacking to receive it. The
nature and manner of what is given to him are vastly different
from what he is accustomed to and desires. Accustomed to his
coarseness and so used to his lowliness, he does not know how
to value such great things nor does he apply his understanding
or will to them.

He is invited to things of the spirit, but he is flesh; he is
called from heaven, but he is earth; he is told to fly, but he
has no wings; life is offered to him, but he always walks with
death; he is invited to blessedness, but he is nothing but misery

---

10. "He is like a tree planted by streams of water that yields its fruit in its
    season, and its leaf does not wither. In all that he does, he prospers"
    (Ps. 1:3, ESV).

75

and wants nothing but misery; he is asked for justice, but he is a captive of sin and finds comfort in it; he is commanded to overcome the world, to fight all its phantoms and dangers, but he sees himself weak and unarmed. Since he does not extend to any of these things, he is not attracted to any of them, and he considers them impossible and foreign. To the village where he was born, to the lowness of the lineage from which he comes, to the flesh that has raised him, to the misery of the earth that he is, there his judgment and eyes go. It is necessary to wake this man with great cries and to strengthen him with great effort; to teach him to know himself, and from there to esteem himself with just and holy esteem; to make him know and be certain of the lineage from which he comes, the state from which he fell, the greatness of his inheritance, and the way of his remedy, so that in some manner he may become attached and yearn for it.

For everything, it is essential to have a guarantee of great security, with which one can sustain oneself and be somewhat certain that what is promised is indeed true. This is the word of God, which He has given and affirmed to humanity. It has been repeated, affirmed, and confirmed many times with great assurances, with great emphasis, with many pledges, so strongly asserted and sworn, because divine mercy understands the great weakness of humanity and the unfamiliarity it has with Him and His matters.

I do not wish to delve further into this, but rather apply it to the purpose of our current discussion. We promise humankind blessedness, and that from this moment, one can begin to be blessed. We advise them to avoid the counsel of the wicked, the path of sinners, and the seat of scoffers; to love the law of God and to meditate on it day and night.

To all this, one might respond that they do not know the

way to be blessed; that the bad counsel comes from their neigh-bors and friends, and from within their own heart; that the path of sinners is very common and there is no other; that if they do not sit in the seat of scoffers, they will be left standing, tired, and mocked by others; that the law of the Lord is very harsh and it is too long a time to spend day and night on it; that they would lose many things that are very important to them; and above all, that even if they decide to follow these things, who will assure them that they can succeed and carry them out? If they do not follow the counsel of the wicked, the wicked will treat them very poorly; if they do not go along the path of sinners, they will tread a very arduous path and encounter great dangers; if they avoid the seat of scoffers, they will find no pleasure in the world and will be forced to live very sadly. If they follow the will of the Lord, they will find many enemies who will persecute and mistreat them: by day, mani-fest dangers; by night, phantoms and shadows that will keep them always in fear and anxiety. They will lose their wealth, their honor, and their life; they will not succeed in what they begin, and they will end up unfortunate, losing both this world and the next.

In order for man to be assured that, if he so desires, he can achieve salvation, and if he fails, it will be his own fault, the Prophet interposes God's promise, on His behalf and with His spirit, affirming that there is a remedy for all this. He offers and assures it as firmly and certainly as the justice and truth of God are firm and certain. The man we discuss will be like a tree planted by streams of water, yielding its fruit in season, whose leaf does not wither, and who prospers in all he does.

While we live on earth and are so accustomed and habit-uated to its ways and things, divine clemency condescends to speak to us and teach us through earthly manners and comparisons. Only one condition is requested of us: that, since these crude comparisons are provided for the crudeness of our judgment, our faith awakens and rises to consider the greatness of the promises, elevating them from the meagerness of earth to the greatness of heaven; from the misery here to the richness there, and from what men and other creatures give and can do, to what God, the Creator and Lord of all, gives and can do.

This comparison, likening the just man to a green and beautiful tree, is very frequent in Divine Scripture. The just shall flourish like the palm; he shall grow like a cedar in Lebanon (Psalm 92). In the Book of Songs (7), it is said that the stature of the spouse is likened to the palm, among many other examples that could be cited.

Now let us explain the reason for the comparison, and then apply it to the blessed man, who is named and given the office of blessed because he is righteous. Among the things we have here, a tree is a very beautiful thing, and there is no one who does not delight in seeing it and does not turn their eyes to it. Imagine, then, a tree whose roots are nourished by streams of water that never dry up throughout the year, which is very green, healthy, and full of leaves; it is certain that this tree will be expected to bear good fruit. These particular conditions are set to better understand the comparison. We say it should be a tree planted by streams of water, one that has leaves all year round, for these are the trees that ordinarily require water. Such a tree will have a great advantage over all other trees, for the others are uncertain if they will have water or not. They depend on rain from the sky; this is uncertain, and it is unknown if or when it will occur. At one time of the year, they will have leaves, at another, they will not; sometimes the leaves will be green, other times they will be dry or wilted; one year, they will bear fruit, another year, they will not; sometimes good fruit, other times damaged fruit; and it is likely that today you will find them with one disease, tomorrow with another, and when you feel most secure, you will find them dried up.

The situation is quite the opposite with the other tree: it has a secure supply of water; whether it rains or not, it cannot lack sap, for the streams from the springs flow by where it is planted. Its leaves never fall, because it has that nature and never lacks water to keep them always green and beautiful; the fruit is certain, because there is no deficiency from heaven or earth that could cause it to be otherwise.

In this manner, our Prophet says that the man who, distancing himself from bad counsel, bad paths, and all other evils, falls in love with the law of the Lord and meditates on it day and night will be like a tree that, although planted on the earth, has perpetual streams of favor from heaven. Just as a tree in the field with streams running right next to it has water exactly where it needs it most and where it benefits it the most—at the roots—so too does the righteous person have streams of heavenly favor to strengthen and support the roots upon which he is founded: faith, hope, charity, and all other divine gifts.

Here, you should understand the water as the favor of the Spirit of God, which in Divine Scripture is represented by water, just as the righteous person is represented by a tree. The greatest need of the earth is water; without it, the earth quickly becomes dry and barren, everything withers and perishes, there is no sustenance for plants, animals, or humans, and from dry land, nothing but poisonous things, diseases, and pestilence are expected. On the contrary, water refreshes and gladdens everything, making it green again and bringing it to life, giving things a new appearance and new existence. There is no better comparison in the world for the Spirit and favor of heaven, sent through Jesus Christ, the Redeemer and Lord of men, for their remedy and renewal.

Thus, to signify the good of the Redeemer's coming, the prophet Isaiah (35) states that the dry place shall be turned into a pool and the parched land into springs of water; in the habitation of dragons, where each lay shall be grass with reeds and rushes. And elsewhere: I will pour water upon him that is thirsty and floods upon the dry ground: I will pour my Spirit upon thy seed, and my blessing upon thine offspring (44). Inviting and exhorting the faithful to come and receive the gifts of the Holy Spirit, he says (55) to come and take water, thereby indicating both the greatness of the misery in which men were and the remedy that was to come to them. They are like dry land, without fruit and life; what comes to them is renewal, refreshment, and abundance.

Returning, then, to our verse, it says that such a man will be like a tree planted by streams of water, indicating the great liberality that the hand of the Lord will use towards him. It does not say that he will be given water drawn from somewhere or brought from afar; not that he will be watered by hand, which might lead to scarcity, nor that it will be at one time more than another; but that there will be streams of water for all times and with great abundance. It is fitting that we consider this matter more slowly. We begin by saying that the roots of the righteous man are founded in the law of God and in obedience to His commandments, and that the roots are faith, hope, and charity, and all the other gifts necessary to contradict and resist all that is in enmity and conflict with divine law and justice and with the blessedness of man. These roots are a favor from heaven and are sustained by it.

The streams of water also symbolize the providence and care that God has over the righteous to protect and deliver them from all the troubles and dangers of this world, so that they neither perish nor suffer harm nor find any impediment to their blessedness. It is explicitly stated that this tree is planted and not self-sown, like others produced by the earth without human industry or hands. This being planted refers to divine election, which is the true foundation of the righteous and the true security of their blessedness. It has no other foundation or reason but the divine will alone, which does with its creatures as it pleases; for God is their Lord and Maker, and as such, He can make use of the works of His hands.

What remains in your charge is that, for greater security and peace of your conscience, and to have a certain assurance of being chosen by God, you must bear fruit in your works, as is fitting for one chosen by God and planted by His election (2 Peter 1).

In all that we have said, it has been declared what are the signs and works of the blessed and righteous man, and in what manner he is favored and assisted by heaven. For he would not do such works if he did not have such favor and streams of water, nor would he have such favor if he did not apply himself to it, take joy in attaining and possessing it, and bear fruit and do works according to such assistance. It is easy to understand from what we have said what is the first and principal condition of the righteous: this is humility and true self-knowledge, for he did not plant himself, but was planted; he would be sterile and unprofitable if he did not have streams of water, which are not from himself, but come and are directed from afar.

This consideration is greatly necessary for the man who wishes to serve God and engages in such exercise: to know that before he could do good or evil, he was chosen and appointed to be righteous, and therefore blessed. This was not because of his works or merits, for many years before he could act, he was chosen. This election will not be fulfilled unless the favor from heaven comes to him for its effect and works. The same who chose him is He who justifies him, He who favors and sustains him, so that, according to the election, he may do works similar to those of His only-begotten Son, for he was chosen and appointed to be conformed to His image (Romans 8).

From this, it becomes clear that the first thing a man must do, with great attention and regularity, is to give thanks to God for choosing him out of His sheer generosity and mercy. One might respond that he does not know if he is chosen, rather he doubts it greatly and is gravely tempted to believe otherwise, and his works bear poor witness. We shall address the matter of works later; for now, we will address the first point.

What one should do is to refer all things to divine goodness and justice, trusting in it with utmost certainty; firmly believing that nothing can be more rightly guided than what divine justice has ordained. Everything else shows great favor; God calls him to diligently seek his salvation. The reason that should convince him of this, persuade him of all this, and enable him to resist temptations, is the very reason presented in the Psalm: seeing oneself planted and born near streams of water. The rationale should be this: divine mercy ordained that he should be born among Christians, among people who have true knowledge of God, where, before he had the understanding to know his good from his evil, or even if he was human or something else, he was baptized, liberated from his captivity, strengthened with God's gifts, received into His friendship and grace, and counted among His children.

Thus, if he had departed from the world at that time, he would have certainly attained heaven and blessedness, and since the Lord did not take him then when he was in His service, it is a sign that He left him to serve Him further, provided he does not flee from His service.

When he grew up and gained knowledge, he found himself near streams of water, in a Christian church, illuminated with light and guidance from heaven, where the revelation of God's Word and the use of His sacraments are present; where His promises and the guarantees of those promises are. He found teachers of everything he needs to know without costing him anything more than his willingness to listen; he is called every day, exhorted every day, strengthened, and disciplined by the Divine Word.

All of these are streams of water, and they are streams from the heavens. What remains but not to flee from them? It is a sign, for they placed me so close that they send them for me; there is no other bad sign than to separate myself by my own will. If I draw near, everything is safe; and to be able to draw near, I am close. I am the judge of my actions; in this alone I must understand. I see that I can do good deeds, and I do bad ones; therefore, I want to take the path, as God says He will judge me by it, in which I see favors, one of them being the unfailing Divine Word that has promised me assistance so that I may act rightly and defend myself from evil. I want to ask, for He will grant it to me, and benefit from it for the things to which I am called.

What we have said is the account that a Christian must make, and all other secrets should be entrusted to the wisdom

of God, relying on His goodness and mercy. With a coura-
geous and joyful spirit, one should endeavor to drink from the
waters that one sees flowing so close. Yet, consider that all the
fruitfulness and all the preparation for bearing fruit are gifts
from another's hand; for he neither planted himself, nor created the water, nor guided its currents. He must acknowledge
that by himself he is not sufficient, not even for a good thought
that would please God. He was conceived in sin and in enmity
with heaven, subject to the law of transgression and evil inclinations. If left to himself, he would be a tree in barren and dry
land, planted only by human hands, bearing fruit of thorns
with worms of the devil and of his own betrayal.

If he is otherwise, it is by the generosity of another, and
by the liberality of the Lord whom he had gravely offended
and who has no need of him, nor of his fruits or leaves. If he is
beneficial, it is for himself; his is the need, and his is the danger. What do you have, man, that you did not receive? And if
you received it, why do you boast and presume as if it were not
given by another hand? (1 Corinthians 4). Consider the danger
you are in, for no matter how great your goods are, the day you
consider them as yours and do not give thanks to the One to
whom they belong, on that very day you will lose them, and if
anything remains of them, it is only the shadow, for your own
pride has left you empty of the true fruit and benefit (Epistle
of St. Jude).

You are so blind and ignorant of the lineage from which
you come, the sin in which you were found, the folly and sickness that you and your roots have endured, that still you are
pursued by thoughts of your vanity, the pride of your madness,
to want to presume that you are what you are not, that you
are worth what you are not worth, that you deserve what you

were given, that others need you, that they owe you and that you earned it. All of these are remnants of your ancient perdition. It is necessary for you to fight against these weaknesses, for no matter how well you are freed, you cannot live without them. The more you are combated, and the more they reside in your heart, the greater your need for resistance and contradiction. You fail to recognize yourself, not because what you should know is not clear and manifest; your eyes are at fault, for otherwise, you would see everything easily. Therefore, strive to open them and, with attentive consideration, examine your blessings and your faults, and you will see that the faults are yours and the blessings belong to another. Look back to what you were and see what a bad tree and what bad fruit you bore. Recognize how much the worm of your vile inclinations pursues you, and you will understand that if there is damage in the fruit, it proceeds from here. Why claim that it comes from the beautiful heaven, that the waters are clear and clean, and that by merely passing through you, they emerge with defects and wrinkles? Consider, as you bear fruit, how little the fruit you give is due to your own fault, your scarcity, and misery; the hand that planted you is generous, the waters that irrigate you are sent in great abundance. Understand that if you are not well provided for, it is not because you were not planted by the waters; but because of the obstacles you seek for yourself, and the laziness you have in wanting to reach them.

All these arguments, and many others that you will find if you wish to look within yourself, truly made without the mix of your flatteries, will conclude against you and will prove your many faults, and will make you recognize your own defects; that you live with greater care, that you understand the blessings you have and from whose hand you have them. They will punish your pride, banish your laziness, and ignite your desire and zeal. Let this suffice to clarify that part of the verse which says that the righteous shall be like a tree planted by streams of water.

Let us now proceed to discuss the fruits of this tree, which must be very similar to its roots and the favor with which it is watered and cared for. We said that the roots were faith, hope, charity, and the other gifts that accompany and adorn these virtues. The favors and irrigation are according to the favor and roots. Thus, it is a sign of the righteous and the blessed that they will bear fruit in their season: just as from a good and healthy tree, well-planted, of good nature, watered with good water, and diligently cared for, fruit is expected in its season with much certainty, so too will this blessed man bear his fruit in his season. What is the fruit? The fruit of faith, hope, and charity. What is the season? The one appointed by the planter.

The sinners we first discussed set their own times for their bad fruits. They bring forth their evil deeds when demanded by their mad judgment and vain wisdom. In this, they follow the whims of their pride, anger, greed, pleasure, and folly. The righteous person has as the season for his fruit that which divine justice demands. Human prudence, confident in itself, its experiences, and its counsel, an enemy of the simplicity of faith, measures and tests its times, being very certain that it will succeed. In some cases, it is very proud, in others very cowardly. This occurs when it is very free and dispassionate in its own judgment. When dominated by the passions and affections we have mentioned—pride and all the rest—it has no other seasons than those of its own affections.

The righteous person, having faith as their principal and primary root, first produces the fruit of faith, which is to trust the timing of all their works to Divine Providence and divine law. Whenever they are commanded to go, they go; they do not know how to make exceptions, they do not know how to argue prudence; day and night, they have no other light or rule but the law of the Lord.

An example of such fruit can be seen in Abraham when he was commanded to sacrifice his son. How many excuses human wisdom would have put forward! That it was not reasonable for him to become the murderer of his own son, that it was against human law and all human inclinations; that what service could the death of an innocent child be to God? Infidelity would have arisen in another guise, with a false color of faith, saying that in this way, the truth of the Lord and the fulfillment of His word, by which He had promised that from the lineage of Isaac would come the remedy for the world, would be impeded. How could this be if Isaac died without offspring? One might dare to interpret the command of the Lord in another way, fulfilling it with some hypocrisy that would be of little cost. Personal interest and paternal affection would resist together; he wanted Isaac as heir and successor to his goods; he loved him as the only son of a legitimate marriage, born in his old age.

All this fell upon Abraham, but faith prevailed in which he was founded, teaching him that there was no other time for his fruits and deeds but that which the Lord and the Author of mercies appointed. Hope also bore fruit, for he did not cease to expect and hold certain that the lineage and offspring of that child would be multiplied like the stars of the sky, like the sands of the sea; that from him would come the blessing of the nations. He had hope against hope, and what human reason took away on one side, the word and truth of God confirmed on the other.

Just as at the beginning, when the son was promised to him, he did not consider his old age nor the sterility and ninety years of Sarah; but held certain what the Lord promised, so later he did not doubt the succession of his son nor the blessing of the world, even though he was commanded to sacrifice him at such a young age (Romans 4). Charity was not sterile there either, for it also bore its fruit as was fitting. He set aside self-love and the love of his son's life for the love that was due to God, and thus he gladly resolved to kill him. This charity also bore true fruit for the son, providing a rule and way to love him rightly, for he recognized how much better it was for that child to die as a sacrifice to the will and obedience of God than to live many prosperous years in the possession and riches of the world.

What you have heard, and in the manner you have heard it, is the time and season in which the righteous man bears his fruit. There are trees that bear fruit in winter but not in summer; others that bear fruit in summer but lack it in winter. Here we take by comparison a tree that never lacks water and always has leaves, so that it has the condition and readiness to bear fruit at all times.

We read in the Gospel (Matthew 21) that as the Redeemer was passing by a fig tree that was very adorned and covered with leaves, He approached it to gather figs, and finding nothing but leaves, He cursed it, and it withered, even though it was not the season for fig trees to have fruit. This causes much amazement, and people seek the reason why our Redeemer cursed the tree that did not have fruit at a time when, according to the rule of nature, it should not have had any. The reason is what you have heard. In that tree, which did not feel and was not capable of injury or punishment, the Son of God taught men that, when He asked for it, how they should bear fruit at all times, and threatened them with the punishment that awaited them if they did not do so. Mercy gives an example of punishment in what does not feel the harm of the punishment. Divine clemency punishes the tree that lacks sense and gives man time and space to turn to Him.

The general rule, then, is that this tree of the righteous does not have within itself the discretion or the choice of the time in which it should bear fruit; rather, it must bear fruit according to the will of the Lord. And just as we taught him to avoid walking in the counsel of the wicked, standing in the path of sinners, or sitting in the seat of mockers—by which we understood all evil actions—and then admonished him to delight in the law of God and meditate on it day and night, meaning at all times and in all his works, so now we tell him to take as his guide for his choices the law and will of the Lord, and to be ready to bear fruit at all times; for he is constantly watered and has perpetual streams of water for this purpose.

All the fruits of trees are similar to their origin and lineage and conform to the virtue and principle they have in their roots. Therefore, we seek the fruits in this manner. The roots are of faith; if they are true, they will produce the fruit of faith. No adversity, no poverty, no labor, no disgrace will be enough to turn back in the confession of the name of God; in manifesting and maintaining His truth; in following His justice and commandments; in remaining and standing firm in them; in believing and being certain that what God says is true; that His promises are infallible; that it is a great mercy He grants; that He guides on the right path; that He will give a prosperous end, and will bring forth victory and great mercies and rewards.

None of these things, nor many others that could be considered, should have the power or be sufficient to hinder the joy that springs from hope; that, in the midst of trials, in the midst of torments, he is consoled by the pleasure of knowing that he will see God, that he will enjoy His company and service forever; that He will bring him joyfully out of all trials and temptations he may face. No need, no bondage should hinder him from having charity with his neighbor; that at all times his heart is open to forgive, love, and pray to God for him; that his tongue is always ready to honor him, his hands to support him, and that the need of others becomes the rule and the season for his fruitfulness.

With these same weapons, may he always conquer the devil and sin. Let his faith be so firm in what God commands that all the interests promised by the devil are not enough to separate him from it. Let his hope be so joyful that he does not exchange his pleasure, the peace of his conscience, or his zeal for the glory of God for all the delights and contentments that sin can bring; may he consider his pleasure to be true and the pleasure of the devil to be ugly, false, and poisonous. Let him have so much charity towards his neighbor that the devil, with all his tricks and schemes, cannot lift his hands or eyes against his neighbor's reputation, honor, property, wife, daughter, or anything else that concerns him.

You have heard about the roots, the fruit, and the time in which it is to be given. Now it is fitting that you hear about the leaves. You know that many trees, after bearing fruit, lose their leaves; there are others that, even after bearing fruit, always retain their leaves as a promise and assurance of the fruit they are to bear. The Prophet alludes to this comparison, saying that the tree to which the righteous man is compared, even after bearing fruit, does not lose or wither its leaves. Through this comparison, God threatens the wicked in Isaiah (1): "You will be like an elm whose leaves wither, and like a garden without water."

Leaves make the tree beautiful, give a good appearance, and bring joy to the onlooker; they are a sign of being well-watered and cared for, and they serve as protection for the fruit. In this way, the righteous man has his leaves—holy displays and holy examples, without causing scandal to anyone. One of the things most fitting for a Christian is to have such composure and such order in his life, in his conversations, in his attire, and in all his actions, that he sets a good example for his neighbor, so that there is never even a suspicion of disdain or scandal that he could give to his brother. For this, he must condescend in many things to the weaknesses of others, even if it means setting aside or adopting practices that are of no consequence to him.

We find many trees that have leaves but no fruit, just as the fig tree when our Redeemer approached it; similarly, there are men with much appearance, who, in their displays, want to make it seem that they have fruit, though they do not. Some of them have their leaves so well-arranged that they can even deceive men; but they cannot deceive Jesus Christ, just as the fig tree did not deceive Him. The wrath He has against them is declared in cursing the tree, causing it to wither instantly. A tree that has fruit but no leaves always proves in the end to be unprofitable.

By these trees, another kind of men, no less vain than the first, is represented. These men wish to excuse the scandal of their lives, their selfish interests, and the freedom they want to take, by claiming a certain inner spirit, a certain special favor from God, a certain holy and good intention, according to them. They wish not to be judged and to judge others, to disdain and excuse what is asked of them and what reason demands from them, pretending not to be like others and claiming particular licenses for not being so. There have always been many such people in the Church of God, and there always will be. Against them, the apostle St. Paul writes in many places, teaching that in everything that God's law tolerates, and that which does not diminish the truth and glory of the Gospel, peace should be kept with men. He could very well eat meat without any offense to God and knew that it mattered very little whether he ate or not what was sacrificed (1 Corinthians 10), and yet he says (1 Corinthians 8) that if he saw that his brother was scandalized by it, he would refrain from eating it for the rest of his life.

"It is good," he says, "not to eat meat or drink wine or to do anything that causes your brother to stumble or be scandalized or weakened." You say that you have faith and that you know what is necessary and what is not necessary, what is relevant and what is not; you have said well, keep that faith and certainty to yourself and before God, but in outward appearances, have consideration and respect for the weakness of your neighbor (Romans 14). In the case of fulfilling the commandment of God to which we are outwardly bound, there is no respect for the powerful or weak, wise or ignorant, nor is there life or death for which it should be neglected: in all other things, great considerations must be given to the peace and tranquility of the conscience of the brother, and in many things, a man must consider it good to lose his contentment and freedom for the sake of the consciences and judgments of others.

The Apostle had great freedom, for he had the freedom of the Gospel and the freedom of its spirit, which he understood very well. Yet, he says (1 Corinthians 9) that although he was free from all, he made himself a servant to all to win more people; he became like a Jew to win the Jews: to those under the law, he became like one under the law, to win those under the law. Great is the freedom that the Gospel permits, but greater consideration must be given to ensure that the freedom of the spirit does not lead us to follow the freedom of the flesh, a deception that has always been very harmful in the Christian Church.

Continuing with the leaves of our tree, I say generally that each person in their state and vocation must always be not only with fruit but also with leaves—green and of good appearance; and it is a great deception for someone to excuse their freedom or what they want to do by saying that they produce the fruit of certain and true works and do not need leaves. The difference in the vocation each one has will cause that—although in the fruit they produce they may be similar to all others—in the leaves, there will be some difference; but all must have fruit and all must have leaves.

One who sees themselves called to the office of the Word of God must not only be content with doing the works they should, like any other, which is the fruit they greatly need for themselves; but they must also have leaves for everyone else, without which they cannot excuse themselves by saying that they bear fruit for themselves and need nothing more. "If I preach the Gospel," says the Apostle (1 Corinthians 9), "I have nothing to boast about; for necessity is laid upon me, and woe to me if I do not preach the Gospel!" For such a person, the leaves will be the doctrine and all the other diligence that they must have for life and word according to their office.

The prophet Ezekiel (47) mentions these trees in the vision where the city of Jerusalem is represented, understood to be the Church. Among the many things he saw, one was the stream of water that flowed from the sanctuary, continually growing toward the East. On both sides of this stream, he says, there were trees with much fruit, which bore fruit every month, and their leaves were for healing. This stream is the flowing waters we have discussed, proceeding from the sanctuary, which is the presence of God. The continuous growth signifies the abundance of mercy and the generosity with which it is communicated to us. The trees on both banks are the righteous. That they grow on both sides signifies that the word and divine mercy are not sterile but find in men those in whom they can produce their effect with great power and efficacy.

The fruit represents good works and adherence to the law of God, which is said to be food, the food that Christ our Redeemer hungered for when, after speaking with the Samaritan woman, He told His disciples that He had a certain food they did not know about (John 4). The leaves are the displays and good examples, which we have said are for the healing of the sick. There is no greater remedy for the proud than the example of the humble; none for the injurer than the patience of the injured; no greater affront or lash for the deceiver than the goodness and simplicity of the righteous. "If your enemy is hungry," says Solomon, "give him food to eat, and in doing so, you will heap burning coals on his head" (Proverbs 25), shaming him with your actions and provoking him to follow virtue through your good example.

For the unbelievers and foreign nations, the leaves of the Christian people are the remedy if they are as they should be.

But due to our sins, if a Moor or a Turk were to enter now, having no knowledge of the truth of our doctrine but wanting to judge by what he saw in us, the certainty of the law we follow, what remedy would he find in our leaves when he saw our pride, heard our foolishness, experienced our vengeance, recognized our superstitions, understood the practice of our lies, our dishonesty, our greed, and our thefts, the profanation of sacred things, the blasphemy and contempt for the very religion we claim to hold? There is no doubt that he would judge unfavorably of the great truth that God has revealed to us, deceiving himself and leading others astray. And we would be, and are, the cause of all these deceptions; and it is evident in the punishments that have come from the divine hand, how much we have offended His Majesty with this sin, giving such a bad odor in the world from the goods and mercies He has granted us above all other men.

Let us now leave this and turn to what we owe one another, and the way in which we repay each other, since we will not concern ourselves with foreign nations. In every state, the leaves represent what each person generally or particularly owes in the displays and signs they give to others. If this rule is true, how inexcusable many will be who claim to be Christians, who, even if we do not judge them by their deeds and observance of the commandments, at least make great efforts—and we know they do—to not have good leaves! Words are leaves, activities are leaves, clothing and personal adornments are leaves, and many other things and ways of living are leaves. The license taken in all this, the looseness and excess, has reached such extremes that from afar or near you will not find leaves as our Psalm requires, no good appearance or color; only dry and sad trees (Epistle of St. Jude), which nevertheless insist that they are laden with fruit and need nothing more.

If we want to focus on the majority of words and conversations that are used, most are filled with pride, threats, fierceness, folly, and shamelessness. And if all this is not clear to the blind, it certainly is to those who see, even if they are short-sighted. This is what resonates through the streets, what is discussed in conversations, where the least inconvenience and the best leaf that can be found in this case is that they are idle words and not vicious ones. What conversation exists now that is not detrimental to the neighbor who hears it, or a display of vanity and folly for the one who speaks it? Or that does not give rise to vile thoughts, foolish and vain plans, and evil actions?

The conversation of the Christian must be holy in all things; great meekness must be present in their dealings; their words should exhort, their displays should strongly rebuke those who stray, even if their tongue does not speak. Finally, in everything that their brothers might judge externally, they must make a representation that testifies they are a creature and workmanship of God, illuminated by the word of His only begotten Son, and zealous for His glory.

These are the leaves we speak of, which serve for the eyes of others and for the preservation of good fruit. The owner of the tree may be content if his plant bears good fruit and will not be overly concerned with the leaves; but the passerby wants good shade and a pleasing appearance. The owner of the tree is God, who knows your heart, and you also, in some measure, know it; with Him and with yourself, as far as the fruit is concerned, you have a final account. He is the witness of your faith, of the simplicity of your heart, and of the purity of your works.

He says with this that you were not planted for Himself alone; for if that were the case, He would have planted you in a secluded corner where only He would see you and only He would enjoy you. Take heed that He placed you in the public field and the public garden of the world, and that He not only desired your fruit but also that you would give recreation, pleasure, and contentment to those who look upon you with your leaves and shade, and give them occasion to bless the Lord who planted you.

It may seem that I have dwelt much on this, insisting and repeating the same ideas, because I know that even with all this insistence, you may not understand, or at least you may not want to understand. And since I have already fulfilled what seems to be my obligation, it is fitting that we leave this, so we can continue with what remains to fully explain the verse.

But first, before we finish this part, it is well that you know the qualities of the leaves that grow on our tree, which are not only not to fall but also not to wither. This is also implied by the Hebrew term. A leaf that does not wither or lose color does not fall. What does this mean? It means that this zeal and care for a good appearance must not falter or slacken in a good Christian. Just as there is diligence for the fruit, there must be diligence for this as well. It further means that this tree we discuss is always in the same state. For the true Christian, what is fitting for his fruit and leaves at one time according to the state of his vocation is the same thing that is fitting at another time, unless charity teaches him something better. It would be a long process if we wanted to go through this in detail for all states and explain what leaves each one in their profession should have and how they should not fall or lose their color. However, there will be no one who truly desires to put his will into keeping the law of the Lord, for whom this very desire will not be enough to teach him all that remains to be taught here due to the brevity of time.

There is one thing in which all must agree, which is a general rule and doctrine for everyone, and that is the external obedience to the Church, designated for the order and unity of the faithful, for the conformity and teaching of its doctrine, for the example they must set for one another and together for the unbelievers, and for the administration and participation of the sacraments.

These are the leaves of holy and true religion, which in the true Christian presupposes true fruit, and the same fruit desires and demands them for its companionship and preservation. Among these things, some are of greater necessity and importance than others, but none are so insignificant that they do not require great respect for the scandal of the neighbor and the demonstration of the obedience that each one must show. You should not understand here that a Christian is obligated to follow the inventions that anyone might want to invent and introduce; we must consider the Church, for it is our mother, our teacher, and to it, we owe particular obedience, and no one should have the audacity to, by the invention and guidance of their own mind, assume the authority of the Church, and demand and teach new obligations to the faithful, nor should they accept them as such.

In concluding with our verse, I say that just as no contradiction or adversity is sufficient to prevent the true Christian from bearing the fruit he is obligated to have in his heart at the proper time, likewise, nothing is enough to cause him to lose the leaf of his outward profession and the example he must set as a tree bearing true and certain fruit. I say that not only must this leaf not fall, but it must not wither or change color; this means he must never show signs of weakness or turn back from what God commands him to do.

The saints, martyrs, and confessors were always accompanied by this leaf; with it, those great men who were tested and exercised with many and varied trials and temptations remained ever green. God not only wants them to bear fruit and serve Him but to do so joyfully. There is no reason for the leaf on the holy tree of the righteous to fall or wither; it always has water, shelter, and favor. Why should it not always have a beautiful leaf? Trees that lack water may understandably be sad and without leaves and fruit at times, but the tree that is always and equally favored should never be without them.

It is well to understand now that in what we have said, there is both a promise from God and what the righteous man must do. I say that these very words: "He will be like a tree planted by streams of water," etc., are a promise from God to him and a demand for what he must do for God. The Lord says that He will favor him and take care of him so that he always has the means to bear fruit when it is required of him, and so that his leaf will never fail or wither; and He demands that he correspond in such a way that he is never found without fruit and never found without a leaf.

The favors from God, as we have already said, are faith, hope, and charity, and these are the roots of the tree; the fruit and leaves of these roots are what is required of him, which is the execution of works of faith, hope, and charity; and this requirement is a great favor, for it helps him to do so. God plants these roots in the chosen and in those who feel the need for them, seek them with great desire, and ask for them with great anguish, asking the One who has them. These are always sustained with streams of continuous favors for those who do not wish to lose them and recognize that in having them, they have blessedness, and in the moment they lack them, they are slaves to perdition and misfortune. The favor that sustains them most is the exercise of these virtues; the occasions for their exercise are favors from God. Every time a man finds himself awakened or forced to, if he does not want to be lost, perform acts of his faith, strengthen and affirm his hope, and communicate and benefit others with his charity, it is a stream coming from heaven for the sustenance of his roots, for the fertility of his fruit, and for the beauty and multiplication of his leaves. In the case of material plants, many succumb to the injuries of time; winter is their adversary, and they lack the power to avoid being battered and stripped of everything.

The trees of our righteousness possess a condition wherein what may appear to be adversity on one side becomes prosperity and irrigation on the other. The devil works to bring them down, and they seek help from God, the Lord of the garden and the one who planted them there and to whom the fruit is due. He favors them in such a way that what seems to be winter becomes their summer. They emerge from such trials with their roots more firmly established, their fruit more abundant, their leaves more beautiful, and with greater readiness and strength for the future. For the devil does not contend with them alone but with the Lord who favors them and sends the streams, and He never fails when His own call upon Him. "The LORD is near to all who call upon Him, to all who call upon Him in truth" (Psalm 145). He who truly knows his weakness and places certain and firm confidence in the divine word and promise will call upon Him in truth. If men exercised themselves day and night, as our Psalm says, in the Word of God, they would have His counsel at hand, His examples continuously before them, His wonders well understood, and His mysteries frequently pondered; and it would be impossible not to become so attached to it or to fail to understand so much of divine goodness and mercy that in their trials and adversities they would not recognize God's favor and mighty hand and the paths by which He leads them to blessedness.

For such people, injury is not an adversity, nor is poverty, persecution, illness, or death. From the world and the devil, who always seeks to understand these things, they are barrenness for good trees, frosts to destroy them and leave them without fruit or leaf; but from God, who cares for them and has promised His favor, they are growth for their roots and improvements. God is faithful, who will not allow you to be tempted beyond what you are able to bear; but with the temptation will also make a way of escape, that you may be able to bear it (1 Corinthians 10). He is so exceedingly faithful that He measures the temptation not just with the strength we have but with the strength He adds to us. Most of the resources are His, and all the profit is ours; He seeks honor in favoring us and in making us victorious if we seek His glory in fulfilling His commandments.

There is nothing in the world that can happen to a man, that if he walks in the law of God, he will not understand and experience as streams from heaven, to make him more fruitful and to store up more treasure in his blessedness. The poor who need your wealth, the persecuted who need your favor, the truth for which you suffer, the toil that seeks you out, are tests of your roots; occasions for you to bear fruit, and if so, they are streams from heaven. There is no reason to turn away from them, for they require what they have given you, give what they have promised you, ask for what you have promised, and add to what you have.

The cross is often a certain companion of the righteous in the world. With this, the world tends to repay the justice it abhors; with this, it takes vengeance on the truth by which it is affronted. This is the last effort with which the devil seeks to uproot the good from the obedience and inheritance of the Lord. And since he and the world are united in this endeavor and are such great artificers, the trials faced by the righteous, if they wish to remain righteous while in the world, are also very great. But God delivers them from all, and He delivers them with such victory that they become more blessed, and the world and the devil are more defeated and more disgraced, for this is the greatest injury with which the Lord seeks to punish them.

The means and instrument by which God affronts the devil and the world are the righteous, when they emerge victorious in adversity and temptation. An example of this is found in Job, whom God set against all the power and vigilance of Satan (Job 1). Thus, the devil, feeling affronted by being defeated by the righteous, in despair of his own strength, flees from him, as the Apostle says: "Resist the devil, and he will flee from you" (James 4).

It remains now to speak of the last condition that the tree of our comparison has: this is that everything it does will prosper. Great is this promise, in which David, with the spirit of heaven, in the name and with the word of God, affirms that everything in which the righteous set their hands will have a prosperous end. This prosperity is not understood nor can it be known by the judgment of the world; we must penetrate and understand it with the eyes of faith, for which it is very clear. The moment we have certainty in our hearts that the power of God is with us to favor us, that His wisdom guides us and

His mercy seeks us, we can be sure that everything we do will prosper and bring great gain. The one who follows the law of God must be certain of the first, from which it follows that the second is an infallible and unfailing rule.

If man were the one handling his own affairs, he might justifiably doubt whether they would have a prosperous or adverse outcome; but since God is the one handling them, how can there be such doubt? "If God is for us, who can be against us?" (Romans 8). Imagine there were a certain kind of merchandise in which gain was assured no matter the route taken, and in no way could there be a risk of loss; that if it were to sink in the sea, the owner would gain much by its sinking; if it arrived safely at the market, he would gain much; if enemies robbed it, if it were consumed by worms, or if it were damaged in any way, great gain would accrue. No matter the news, the merchant would rejoice and give rewards to the messenger, knowing for certain that great treasures were being directed his way. This is how the affairs of the righteous are when placed in the hands of God.

Lord and my God, says our Prophet elsewhere, in your hands are my fortunes (Psalm 31). If they were in other hands or in mine, I would live in fear whether they would turn out well or badly; but being in your power, in your knowledge and mercy, I am certain of a good outcome. My good fortune lies in no more than my desire to place my fortunes in your hands, and to be content with it, for whatever comes, I am certain of good fortune. From your hand comes illness; if I choose to recognize that it comes from you and accept it as such, great are the riches and good fortune that my illness brings me; if health comes, riches come with health. If you, Lord, will that I be poor, great are the treasures hidden in this poverty; if you permit me to be rich through the path of your commandments, the treasures of poverty are transferred to wealth. You placed me in a state of honor, I live securely knowing that great and prosperous ends are guided here; I live affronted and persecuted in the world, therein lies my gain. I have food on earth, it will bring me profit; I come to die of hunger, the same gain I have. I die of illness, great are the riches hidden in this death; you left me with life, for great goods you leave me alive.

Finally, he who entrusts his fortunes to the hand of the Lord cannot escape without gain. The way to place them in His hands is by keeping His commandments, with certain and firm faith that divine providence and mercy guide him to a prosperous end. In these hands, the Apostle St. Paul placed his fortunes, finding everything good. "I know how to be humbled," he says, "and I know how to abound; in everything and in all things I have learned both to be full and to be hungry, both to abound and to suffer need: I can do all things through Christ who strengthens me" (Philippians 4).

We should not be surprised that the great friends of God, mentioned in Divine Scripture, received such great mercies in the favors of this life and the next, and obtained such great testimony from the mouth of the Lord who favored them; for they entrusted their affairs to the will and hand of God, with the utmost faith that, not deviating from the fulfillment of His commandments and with their hearts devoted to this, never following other paths or counsels, everything would prosper greatly for them.

The successes and good fortune of Abraham proceeded from this root: he never doubted his happiness and the joyful outcome of his labors, even though he found himself in a foreign land, persecuted by Canaanites, driven away and exiled again by great hunger; deprived of his wife, without legitimate offspring to inherit his patrimony and the great hope of his lineage. As he entrusted everything to the goodness, mercy, and divine promise, everything turned out prosperously. To the great poverty and misery in which he lived for so many years in the land of Canaan, succeeded great authority, great abundance of riches and goods in the same land. His wife was restored to him, with great fear that God placed in those who took her; he achieved victory over his enemies; in the extremeness of old age and the barrenness of Sarah, he received a son of blessing, from whom the blessing of all nations would come.

By this same path was guided the prosperity of Jacob: in Syria, his children and wealth multiplied, he emerged joyful and victorious from Laban's persecution, found Esau's anger softened, and gained peace and favor with him; at the end of his labors, he died prosperous and honored in Egypt, surrounded by all his children and a great multitude of his descendants and lineage.

From this same root came the great status and command of Joseph who, after the danger of death his brothers intended for him, after being sold by them, and enduring persecutions and imprisonment in Egypt, became such a powerful prince, the sustainer of all the land and his own people. Through this path, Job's prosperity was restored, with double the wealth he had lost, God giving him such sons and daughters anew, making him so distinguished and renowned in the regions of the East, and granting him many years of life.

From here, our prophet David found his deliverance from his labors and affronts, being delivered many times from the hand and persecution of Saul, achieving so many victories over his enemies, being restored to the possession of his kingdom, and being pacified and confirmed in it. Even after his death, his memory held such value before the Lord, in whom he placed his trust, that although his descendants were so wicked and harshly punished, in the midst of these punishments, God said that for David's sake He did not wish to end his lineage or remove it from the possession of the kingdom; His will was that there would always be a burning candle and a man from that lineage to be king and sit on David's throne, in proof and memory of the great faith and friendship he had with him.

These holy men were gravely tempted, tested with great rigor, and accompanied by harsh crosses; their great prosperities had significant beginnings, means, and mixes of adversity, but they had such great faith and constancy in all, that they never strayed from God's commandments. Rather, they confirmed themselves more in them and repented deeply for any instance that even slightly made them falter. They were certain that if they did not depart from the Lord's will, He would never cease to act according to His nature. They attributed adversities to their own faults, seeing them as light punishment for the greatness of their sins. They understood all this as the merciful discipline of a most compassionate Father who wanted to correct them and provide a restraint so they would not be lost. Their flesh felt the bitterness of trials and persecutions, desired things according to their tastes, but their spirit was strengthened and found great contentment in the fulfillment of the Lord's will, trusting everything to His hands, always waiting for the outcome His mercy would provide, knowing that from such a good hand, only good fortune could come.

The prosperities that occurred did not bring them as much joy for their own sake, for they were prepared for greater labors, but rather because they happened to know men would see how good a Lord they followed, how friendly He was to His friends, how certain and true in His promises, and that, attracted by these gifts, men would begin to understand His greatness and gradually be awakened to understand how wise it was to fully trust in Him. For this reason, Divine Scripture sets them as examples of what men should do for God and who God is for men.

Whoever wishes to imitate their faith should not demand an outcome that necessarily has the appearance of prosperity in this world. He should not measure himself by David's kingdom, Abraham's wealth, or the multiplication of Job's goods. The moment he stubbornly wishes to imitate them in this, he no longer imitates them in faith; nor would they cease to be faithful even if it never happened to them; and it did not happen this way to all the faithful, nor was the prosperity they achieved in this life equal to the crosses and torments with which they were tested.

The spiritual man should conceive a very different sentiment from such examples. The Lord would give us time to discuss this another day. For now, it suffices to extract from this a rule for the man who wants to be a Christian and for a true explanation of the verse from our Psalm. The first thing he should do is to take as a certain and universal rule for his blessedness the keeping of God's law and the fulfillment of His will. While he remains in this life, for his own remedy and for those in his charge, he should use the means that the same law and divine Providence have taught and permitted him. He will avoid tempting God and will always remember that he lives in a land of toil and cross, and that it is against the pronounced sentence that by the sweat of his brow he shall eat bread (Genesis 3).

He should never accept help or advice that is not in accordance with the Divine Word, neither for life nor for death nor for all the goods or evils that can happen to a man in this life. When he has established this in his heart and asked God for favor to carry it out, the second thing he must do is to conceive a true faith and a very sure and firm hope that everything will turn out well for him and that all his matters will have a joyful and prosperous outcome; that by approaching God, the source of all good things, good fortune cannot escape him. The third thing he must do, and which is the key to everything, is not to become the judge of his prosperity or adversity, nor of his goods or evils; he should only be concerned with the study and diligence he puts into keeping the Lord's law, considering the esteem he holds for it within his heart, and how enamored his soul's eyes are with its beauty. For this, he must enter into judgment with his own conscience and hear from it the friendship or enmity he has with sin. With this law, he should measure all his works and thoughts; in everything else, he should not intervene, but trust everything to God's will, taking only the light of His commandments as his guide.

Great is the pride of the miserable man who dares to set limits for such a great Lord concerning the manner of his prosperity, who wants first to show Him the form of the goods he needs, so that by that measure He may send them. Foolish man, what wisdom do you possess to advise God? What goodness can you point to that is not misery and scanty compared to the source of such great goods? What can your poverty ask for, even when you extend yourself greatly, in the face of the treasures of that infinite power? What can you desire or want for yourself that is not far greater in the hands of the mercy of the Lord who created and redeemed you, and who wants to show who He is in what He does for you? How much better you would do if, distrusting yourself, you fled from your judgment and remained silent, so that your folly and scarcity would not destroy your goods, and you trusted entirely in Him who wishes to employ His wisdom to guide you, His power to favor you, His treasures for your wealth, His goodness to communicate it to you, His justice to cleanse you, His mercy so that you may have victory against your enemies!

Great is the contradiction that man has for all this, great resistance must be in him, and he needs heaven's favor; he must ask for it regularly and it will not be denied him. When he feels the powerful hand of God with him, let him take advantage of such help to achieve such a great victory. The world despises such men: it is clear, it considers them mad and lost; but how much greater reason they have to consider the world as lost, lost without remedy!

I want to ask them one thing. If it were the case that you were dealing with very important business and merchandise and at the same time you were so ignorant that you neither knew currency nor understood accounting nor comprehended subtleties, and you had as adversaries in your profit and wealth men of the sharpest intellects, great tricks, and great deceptions, let us suppose with this that you had a father who loved you excessively, who had the greatest desire for you to do well in your business, and who put all diligence to this effect; who was extremely expert and supremely knowledgeable in all things, making notable advantage in all kinds of knowledge, not only over your adversaries but over all the rest of the world, and that this father secretly handled all your business and accounts and everything necessary for you, would it not seem that you could walk securely and sleep soundly, as they say, and laugh with great reason at anyone who laughed at you?

Well, this is a proper analogy for what we are now discussing. The foolish world thinks that no one handles the business of the servants of God, that, as if they were ownerless and worthless things, anyone can enter into them and do whatever they want; the world thinks that simplicity is unprotected, justice has no judge, patience has no avenger, truth has no defender; and it lives greatly deceived, for all this has a Lord, and a greatly powerful Lord, who loves and is zealous for it and for those who follow it.

The Christian can indeed sleep securely, knowing that his affairs are in hands that will give them a good outcome. In peace, says our Prophet, I will lie down and sleep; for you alone, LORD, make me dwell in safety (Psalm 4). Everything is for the better and for greater gain for the Christian. Where will man not come out with prosperity, when he comes out with it from the persecution and temptation of the devil, and, as we said above, comes out with greater strength, greater wisdom, and greater mercies?

This prosperity goes further: one gains even from sin, if the sinner wishes to leave it. God's glory is exalted more by forgiving him, for what the Lord values most is forgiving the sinner who seeks Him. The sinner gains greater humility and self-awareness, greater diligence in calling upon God, greater enmity and distrust of his sin, as one who has recognized his deeds and their ugliness, and greater gratitude toward the Lord who delivered him from such evil. Thus, there is nothing from which a man seeking God does not gain a prosperous end. "And we know that all things work together for good to those who love God" (Romans 8).

The disaster and great evil of offending God cannot be exaggerated; but the Lord, though offended, is so merciful that He leads the sinner to repentance, awakens and favors him for it, receives his tears and groans, forgives his sin, restores him to the former friendship, and grants him as many mercies as if he had never angered Him. The sinner who understands this, how much he gains! How beneficial is the punishment that awakened him from his slumber, that made him aware of the Lord's wrath against whom he sinned, that chastened and warned him for the future! "Before I was afflicted I went astray, but now I keep Your word," says David in Psalm 119.

If, from something as lost and unfortunate as sin, the sinner gains merely by returning to God's hands, from which all good fortune flows, what doubt can we have of the good fortune that will come to us if we keep His commandments? What would He deny us who does not deny us forgiveness for having despised Him? How could He forget us in this life who does so much to give us the next? It follows then that if we have a spark of faith, and if under the name of Christians we do not have another religion than that of lost peoples, and do not place our blessedness in what they have placed theirs, we should repent of all our sins, recognizing that they are the true misery and the path to perpetual perdition; these alone separate us from God, provoke His wrath against us, and cause us, creatures made in His likeness, to represent the image of His enemy the devil, in whose company will remain forever those who imitate his deeds and do not heed the voice of the One who calls them not to be lost.

Let us acknowledge how much we are obliged to serve the goodness, meekness, and immeasurable mercy of the Lord, who seeks us for such great good. Let us lodge His commandments in our hearts, living with the certain assurance that all will prosper for us, both in earthly goods and in those of heaven.

The Fourth Sermon

No de esta manera los malos, sino como el polvo que levanta el viento del haz de la tierra.[11]

IN THE PREVIOUS VERSE, we discussed the comparison and likeness of the righteous man to the tree planted by streams of water. We said that in the same words were comprehended the signs of such a tree and the promise of heaven's favors and all that was needed for it to be such. In the following verse, the comparison of the wicked is set forth, the signs they have in this world, the nature of their works, and the threat of being forsaken by divine favor if they persist in their wicked path. The good tree was planted by the hand of God, had perpetual streams of water, bore its fruit in season, its leaf did not wither, and everything it did prospered. The wicked, however, are like dust that the wind drives away from the face of the earth.

This dust mentioned in our Psalm, according to the proper meaning of the word, is a fine substance made from the husks of wheat when it is threshed or from the little pods and coverings of the grain; I believe the farmers call it chaff. This is, as you know, something that the wind easily carries away. Thus, the Prophet took his comparison from something that was green and looked good when the ear was in the field, and shortly thereafter dried up, turned to dust, and was carried away by the wind.

---

11. "The wicked are not so, but are like chaff that the wind drives away" (Ps. 1:4, ESV).

It is well that we continue to contrast the first tree with the dust we are speaking of so that you may understand the great difference between the righteous and the wicked, and the sinner who follows the bad counsel and example and who sits in the seat of scoffers. The tree was planted by the hand of God, had deep roots; this other is planted by another hand, rooted lightly, remains green for a short time, dries up quickly, turns to dust, and is scattered by the wind.

The righteous man places all his trust and hope in being in the hand of God, by which he is sustained and favored; he considers everything else transient and perishable, knowing that all earthly things are subject to change, and thus does not rely on them, nor is he alarmed or despairing when he sees them change. The wicked and lost man is attached to the earth; the deeper his roots in it, the more secure he feels. In it, he plants his honor, his wealth, his pleasures, and his delights. The children of Hagar, says the Prophet, sought wisdom that is of the earth (Baruch 3), like slaves and of low condition, they placed their blessedness in the misery and servitude of the world, failing to recognize or value the freedom of the children of God.

The bristles of the ear of corn appear beautiful and green for a few days, but as the root is light and summer comes upon it, they dry up and fall to the ground, and being trampled and turned to dust, any wind carries them away without leaving a trace. The roots cannot last longer than the foundation on which they are sustained. What is there on earth that, in a man's brief and miserable life, does not undergo a thousand changes? (Ecclesiastes 1). As are the roots of the wicked, so is the water with which they are watered. The unfortunate one lacks streams, all his hope depends on the whims of clouds, not the clouds sent by divine mercy, but those imagined by his vanity. No matter how well things go for him, no matter how prosperous his time is, soon summer will come and take away his fruit, and he will be dust in the wind. This is the miserable irrigation that sustains the wicked: murky, scant, and deceptive, and thus it fails him at the best time. He has no streams from heaven, not because they are not sent, but because he does not want to receive them and makes himself incapable of receiving them.

Of the righteous, we said that he opens the channels through which the favors and streams of heaven enter his heart; the wicked closes them so they cannot enter. The former opens them through the recognition of his own need and by deeply feeling this lack, he asks God for remedy; the latter neither feels his misfortune nor understands the need to seek remedy. These are like those whom Solomon describes as sleeping on the sea, who are mistreated in their dreams and say upon waking: "They struck me, but I was not hurt; they beat me, but I did not feel it" (Proverbs 23).

Such are those who, living amid great dangers, surrounded by their sins, sleep the sleep of false security, like one who sleeps on the sea during a storm and peril. Their unfortunate conscience is so dulled and intoxicated with the wine of their pleasures, interests, and passions that they scorn and forget God's judgment. God punishes them with grave penalties, yet they do not feel it.

What greater punishment can be imagined in the world than for the sinner to be so blind and so carried away that he does not feel the scourge of God, who allows him to remain in such a state? God gives them life so they may convert, extends their time, waits for them, and calls them, and they use this to continue in their misfortune and to keep drinking the wine of their sleep and perdition. No matter how many calls God makes, no matter how many paths He uses to call and invite them, they are so stubborn that they overcome with their wickedness the holy persistence of God. They act as the Prophet says of them: their fury is like that of the serpent; they are like the deaf asp that stops its ear, which does not hear the voice of charmers, no matter how skillful the enchanter may be (Psalm 58).

Compare here the diligence and power with which God calls and seeks sinners to the words and enchantment of the magician who lulls and binds serpents, without anything in the world obstructing him; and the malice of the sinner, to the cunning of the same serpent that remedies it with only one thing, covering its own ears to avoid hearing the enchantment. This is the resistance that the wicked put up against the Word of God, against opportunities, favors, and inspirations from heaven. They make themselves deaf, put obstacles to their attention, and blind their understanding, unwilling to understand what they do understand, always attributing everything to very different ends and hardening their own conscience so that it does not hear the voices or feel the kindnesses or punishments that come from God's hand. Thus, this person is abandoned by the favor of God that he does not want to receive; he is dry and barren land, without moisture and without virtue for good.

For the righteous, we said that opportunities and all things that come their way are irrigation channels from which they take great benefit for the strength of their roots. The wicked and hardened receive no benefit from any of these things, nor do they want to take advantage of them; they delay everything, excuse everything, they are blind. Being so dry and without moisture, it necessarily follows that they lack roots; they neither have complete faith, charity, nor hope; they have neither fruit nor leaf: everything they have is feigned, apparent, and not true, as will clearly appear when we come to the test.

You may ask, why does it seem that such a sinner, being dust as the Prophet says, appears to his own eyes and to the eyes of the foolish world as a tree that is green, with roots, bearing fruit and leaves? To this, I have already responded that all this is fantastic and merely the imagination of him who believes he is a tree, and of those who judge him as such, being dust carried by the wind, as we shall say later.

It remains now to give a more extensive and detailed explanation of our answer. The world has its waters with which it irrigates its wicked and deceptive plants, and gives them that false being: from here comes that those who have no more judgment than what the world itself has given them, deceive themselves and deceive others, believing that what is dust and devoid of all good is a beautiful tree planted by streams of good waters and bearing much fruit.

The waters of the world are compared by the prophet Isaiah to those of Egypt, whom the Lord threatens, saying that the waters of its sea will fail, that its mighty river will be destroyed, and its streams will dry up; the brooks of the fields will wither, the reeds and rushes will perish, the source will fail at the river's mouth; everything sown by the river and irrigated will come to great ruin, and the fishermen and those who cast nets on the waters will mourn; all those who weave fine linen, all who make fishponds will be confounded (Isaiah 19). These are the waters of Egypt: waters of human wisdom and human confidence, of human counsel and intellect, and the industry of their hands. With these, the wicked are watered, and they receive that false appearance by which they are judged to be trees.

The first root of the righteous, we said, is faith: the first and principal root of the wicked is their own wisdom. With this, they govern all their thoughts and actions; with this, they measure and decide the times when they will or will not do their deeds; with this, they guide their prosperity and resist their troubles. The first and main danger of the wicked is their inability to truly believe that everything is guided and well-guided by the hand of God. They are always blasphemous against Providence; they imagine that there is negligence in God and that if they do not correct things with their own counsel, they cannot achieve a good end by the sole path of heaven and by the rule of God. Therefore, whenever things do not go according to their desires, they follow the advice of the wicked and the example of sinners.

They reject and discard all the streams of heaven; they only want to be helped by the lagoons of Egypt. When God gives them the opportunity to do good and help the poor, permitting and guiding them to wealth and the ability to do so, they become more avaricious; they feign greater needs and greater estates; their greed is inflamed, and they impose obligations on themselves to further accumulate their treasures. When they are made poor, so that by this stream of heaven they might humble themselves and bear the cross, and be guided to much and beautiful fruit before God, they then become blasphemous against the divine work; impatient with the cross; robbers, liars, and deceivers, full of a thousand deceptions to remedy their poverty.

They are given health so that, admonished and irrigated with so much water from the hand of the Lord, they might work in this world, lawfully providing for their needs and those of others; so that, through the path of their vocation and the state in which God has guided them, they might be a fruit-ful and beneficial tree for men; but they employ this health in being idle, in living more idly, and from more idleness, more viciously, in beastly delights, in malice, in endeavors, in abom-inable activities for the glory of God and for other men. When illness occurs, whether through their sins or by the hand of God, calling them to patience with this stream, to the recog-nition of their great faults, as a hindrance to their sins and as a reminder of the things of heaven, they place all their care in worldly remedies, in forgetfulness of who they are, of the hand of God, and in blasphemies against Him.

They are placed in a state of honor or dignity, so that, con-sidering this work, they might recognize that they are guided by divine providence, and use their office, power, and influ-ence in the protection and favor of the poor, the alone, and the forsaken; but they become proud and tyrannize the world, unbearable to both the great and the small. God's will guides them to a lowly state, so that they might humble themselves and understand that this was a remedy to avoid the dangers of pride and wickedness; yet they follow the counsel of the wick-ed, the path of sinners, and with great treachery, to the harm of their neighbors and great offense to God, they seek to rise high-er and higher than what God intended and His Word permits.

When he is persecuted in the world, falls into affronts or injuries; instead of drinking the water of this irrigation, suf-fering it with patience, forgiving his enemy, recognizing how much greater things divine mercy has forgiven him, he stokes his own anger and, turning from a man into a wild beast, seeks revenge and the harm of his neighbor by all possible means. His life has been spent in sins upon sins, from which no benefit is derived; he is only given time out of great mercy, calling him to repentance; he postpones this to old age or to a time when he thinks he will be so full of vices that he cannot take more, and, tired of his sins, will either leave them or be left by them.

The wicked also delays all opportunities, flees from all good deeds, is quick to commit all evils; for every good thing, he finds reasons and excuses, for every evil thing, his desire is alive, and his feet are swift. And just as he blasphemes against the providence and mercy of God, so he does against His justice. With duplicity and hypocrisy, he offers things of no value and vain sacrifices, daring to think that divine goodness can be satisfied with the works of his deceptions. This is the first root of the wicked, and this he holds instead of faith. And if he claims to have true faith as God wishes His own to have, we will prove him a liar by his fruits when we come to discuss them, and now he can be proven by his own confession.

Come here, lost and doubly lost man, so bold and shameless, in whom do you say you believe? What is the first article of your religion? If you say you believe in God Almighty, Creator of heaven and earth, do you not see how you lie? If He is almighty, why do you dare to be His enemy and contradict His commandments? If He is almighty, He must also be all-wise, all-good, and all-just. So why, let us see, do you blaspheme against His goodness, mock His wisdom, and seek to satisfy His justice with such false works that even your own, as wicked as you are, would not be satisfied with them? You confess God with your mouth and deny Him with your hands (Romans 2). Why do you not show some sign of what you say you believe? Why do you not walk humbly with Him whom you confess can do so much? Why do you not follow the counsel of Him who knows so much? Why do you not try to please Him who is so good?

These wicked men abandon what they themselves claim is good, and follow what they themselves claim is evil; from which you can infer that they lack the root of true faith, obstruct the streams of heaven, and admit the waters of Egypt, of their own wisdom, of the gratification of their desires, of the false happiness that the world deceitfully offers them.

They also lack the second root, which is charity, because they neither love God nor their neighbor. It is clear that they do not love God since they do not trust in Him; they deceive themselves when they think they love Him. If not, let us take account, and see if they should say in their conscience whether they would be content if another man like them swore that he loved them and, upon experience, found that he did the opposite of what they had entrusted to him; that he took away the estate they had entrusted to him; that he distributed it contrary to how they had instructed; that he defamed their honor and truth and wanted to fulfill with them with false words and deeds. Would they believe that this man loved them? Thus, they are to God.

I have proved, if I am not mistaken, that it is evident that the sinner does not have love for God. Neither does he have love for his neighbor. Because all the love he has is directed towards, and ends, in his own satisfaction. The proof is clear: for at the expense of his brothers, he seeks his own profit or pleasure; and wherever this is not found, he becomes a manifest enemy of his neighbor, or at least a false friend. So, if he has any love for those he calls his friends, it is for the interest and pleasure he derives from them.

If he loves his own child, it is not because God gave him, not because his child will be saved and fulfill God's law, not for the goodness of that child referring to the same goodness; but because it is a piece of his own flesh, and in the same way he loves what remains, and adores its honor, pleasures, and satisfaction; by this same path he loves the part of his flesh that is in his child, and adores the same in it. So, whom will this man have true love for if he does not have it for his own child?

We have brought to light how sinners lack the second root, which is charity. They also lack the third, which is hope. The very fear they have, that there might be a lack in their goods guiding them so contrary to what God commands, takes away all the effect of true hope. In the midst of their prosperities and in the summer of their pleasures, they are agitated by the fear of lack; in nothing do they trust with secure confidence, because they themselves have experienced that what they trust in is subject to great dangers; and for no other reason are they so solicitous and sleepless, it arises from nothing other than their own fear and apprehension. Hence, the wicked never have true joy, never true peace or security. "There is no peace," says the LORD, "for the wicked" (Isaiah 48).

If what they love, what they seek, and what they desire were certain, which is impossible, the very war of their conscience, the testimony of God's law, would be enough for a great conflict, much more so with everything combined. In the abundance and possession of their interests, they fear the lack that will come. In lack, they despair and never have security that they will attain what they seek. Faint in work, agitated in prosperity, good news never enters their heart without being accompanied by the bad, because the opposite of this is characteristic of the hope the righteous have in God, and the Lord does not allow the vain confidence with which the wicked operate to have the signs and effects of that which is placed in Him, nor that they derive from their follies what the righteous achieve through the confidence placed in divine goodness and mercy.

We have proved, in my opinion, that the wicked have no roots, nor is it possible for them to have roots, as they do not have nor wish to have streams of water from heaven. Let us move further and see what fruit they have. Any sensible man would judge that a plant without roots will not bear fruit, and if it seems to have fruit, it will be feigned and as if made by magic, of no value or effect. Instead of faith, they have their own judgment and wisdom, instead of charity their interests, instead of hope their confidences. The roots are feigned and vain, so the fruits will be feigned and vain. The righteous bore fruit not when they chose, they neither had nor wanted to have the choice for it; they bore fruit according to the time God appointed. The wicked, in contrast, never when God commands, but at the time they choose, and this time never comes. The sinner never knows the time or season in which the Lord requires fruit; the time he chooses will never come, nor is it possible for it to come, because the time he chooses is winter, and the time God chooses is summer, and only God knows and measures the summer for bearing good fruit.

The wicked do not recognize the opportunity, nor the time when they are asked to bear fruit; they appeal to wealth, they appeal to poverty; they excuse themselves with honor, they excuse themselves with disgrace; they excuse themselves with health, they excuse themselves with illness; neither the time of pleasures nor the time of sorrows is suitable for them. Each of these times is God's time if one considers His justice and mercy; none of them is suitable for the wicked if one considers their intentions. When will this summer come in which this man will bear fruit? The time he chooses, being feigned, is unsuitable and incapable of bearing fruit, and if he lets God's time pass, it is necessary that he remains barren. In this way, God rebukes His people of Israel through the prophet Jeremiah: "Even the stork in the sky knows her appointed times, and the turtledove, the swift, and the swallow observe the time of their migration; but my people do not know the judgment of the LORD. How can you say, 'We are wise, and the law of the LORD is with us'?" (Jeremiah 8).

Here is demonstrated the great blindness and wickedness of sinners, who, recognizing the birds by the signs of the time when they must go and when they must return, take advantage of this knowledge, and do not delay their departure nor delay their return: they, having the law of God, which designates the times and seasons when they must bear fruit, do not want to recognize it, but rather leave the Lord without it and themselves deceived. Thus, Christ, our Redeemer, weeps over Jerusalem, prophesying its desolation because it did not recognize the time of its visitation (Luke 19). This is what the wicked await and what is precisely for them, since they take upon themselves the task of measuring and designating the time in which God wishes to be served. As they do not discern the time, neither do they discern the fruit; as they do not have true roots, neither is what they bear certain. This will be seen more clearly by the rule of fruits, although it has been seen quite clearly in what we said about the roots. This repetition will serve for you to understand it better and to remember it more if you wish to take advantage of it.

When the sinner is asked for the fruit of faith: that which God's law demands of him is something that serves Him; that, however small it may seem to the world, it is great and highly esteemed in His eyes; that he should not let such an opportunity pass because much will be lost in it; that, in doing so, nothing can go wrong because He takes it upon Himself; if the path seems rough, He goes in his company; if hardship arises, He will provide a good outcome, the wicked respond to all this by choosing another task of their own design, fearing adversity, avoiding hardships, fearing what they should not fear, undertaking and despising what is dangerous. They are offered the pleasures of heaven, but, lacking faith, they neither feel nor become fond of them, nor do they like or desire them. They rejoice in nothing but the ugliness and grossness of the world. As there is no purity in their heart, nothing of a good spirit finds place or lodging in it. All this is a sign of being devoid of true faith and true understanding, for they neither feel who is the Lord who created them nor the paths by which He calls and wishes to guide them.

By another way of examining the fruits, we can recognize how the wicked lack the root of charity, and how in place of it, they have their own evil interests and a false and feigned love for God and their neighbor. Let us look at their actions in their dealings with others and see what motivates them. They seek their own profit in such a way that they shamelessly say, "Why should I be concerned with anything from which I do not gain interest?" They not only seek their own interests but do so with great loss and cost to others. They want everyone else to lose so that they can gain; they want everyone to have less so that they appear richer; they want the honor of others to decrease so that theirs increases; they derive pleasure from the suffering of others.

By our sins, these wicked people we speak of are the least evil if we consider those who openly and as lawless men take away others' honors and estates, without any fear of God or respect for people, manifestly causing destruction and dissipation of other men. This has led to the perception that those who, in all their dealings and everything they encounter, seek their own profit and interests at the expense of their neighbors, are not considered evil as long as they do not rob on the roads or do something equivalent.

Trying to make them understand that these actions are not according to God's law, that they must go much further and do much more for each other, does not lead to their confession, because in their hearts there is no root of charity. And lacking this root, it is necessary not only that they do not bear good fruit but that they never take pleasure in the thought that it would be good to do so. To forgive an injury to their neighbor seems madness to them. To do good to their enemy, they do not think it possible, nor do they find anything pleasing in it. To give alms to the poor—how scantily they do it, with what pain they take from their estate what they are to give, how delayed and with what slowness, how much by carnal affections and prudence, how much for their own contentment rather than for others, because it all ends up being for themselves! And what most concludes their blindness and shows they lack true roots is the thought they have when they have done these things, that they have performed acts of charity.

As such a person does not have the law of God in their heart, nor do they seek counsel from it, they do not test their own actions to disillusion themselves and see how wrong they are. They give with sadness, but God loves a cheerful giver (2 Corinthians 9). They delay and give sparingly, but God wants them to help promptly, and not make their neighbor buy relief with importunities. But why are we wasting time? They are without the root of faith, how could they not be without charity? They do not trust in God, how will they trust in men? They think heaven will fail them, how do you expect them to think that the earth will not fail them?

He does not understand how the Lord acts for him, so how can he act for others? He is not grateful for the blessings of God nor does he recognize that they come from His hand, so how can he be generous in distributing them? He does not want to consider how, being such a wicked man, divine goodness gives him time for repentance and to obtain forgiveness for his sins, so how can he have the heart to forgive his neighbor? He has neither humility nor understanding of what he is or what he owes, so how can he act with true humility and true understanding?

If he does anything for his neighbor, or any deed comes from his hands that seems charitable, it has a false name and a false appearance. It is not guided by the law of God, but by his own judgment; not by the divine commandment, but by his own interest; not by obedience to the Lord, but by his own satisfaction; not by true love for his neighbor, but by his carnal affection; not by the glory of heaven, but by his own; not by the humility and silence of charity, but by the proclamation and display of his vanity and pride. These are the fruits he bears when he bears them; and as the roots are, so are the fruits.

The fruits of hope are no less lacking because if it is not with him, neither will its fruits be. We began by saying, if you remember well, and now we will say more clearly, that the effect of hope is a joy in the work, a fortitude in the labor, a vision that, though distant, indicates its destination; a certainty that all this will reach a prosperous end and fulfillment of what is promised. The wicked lack all this, and necessarily so.

No matter how much the world delights him, the very changes he fears make him sad; and it is for no other reason that he puts so much effort into his affairs, but for the great fear he has. The further he goes, the more his fear grows. If he remembers God, he sees how he loses Him; if he thinks of the world in which he trusts, he fears it as well; if he considers his age, he sees it ending; if he contemplates his treacheries, he fears they will be discovered; if he considers the account he must give, he knows the remedy he has; if the repentance of his sins, he finds them deeply embedded in his heart; and he still lost because of his sins.

These are the fruits that the wicked man bears for himself and his master. Let us move further and consider the leaves, for as the fruits are, so will they be. There is no remedy here but that they will be of very poor color: and if they seem good, it will be hypocritical and false. What can the wicked serve in the world but to bring shame to their Creator, infamy to the law of God, hindrance to all good, an invitation to evil, harm to men, and deceit to the world? This is the work of his pride, of his treachery, of his revenge, of his pleasures and baseness, of his hypocrisy, and his false appearance of good.

A plague on the earth, such is the wicked man, and like a plague, he spreads to others and dissipates health. One proud man makes a thousand proud; one avaricious, a thousand avaricious; one envious, a thousand envious; one carnal, ten thousand carnals; and one hypocrite, as many hypocrites. He does harm not only with his vices but also spreads these very vices; his sin kills the subject it falls upon and is contagious to others. They are enemies to each other and collectively enemies to the good. Just as the leaves of the righteous served as medicine, so the leaves of the wicked bring disease; just as the former glorify

God, so the latter show disrespect and blaspheme His majesty.

The entire righteous tree is filled with good, all bearing fruit, all with leaves; all joyful for itself and joyful for others. The entire wicked tree is filled with evil; dry and sad for itself, and dry and sad for others. In the former, everything he did had a prosperous end. In the latter, everything goes from bad to worse, from disaster to disaster. He has bad roots and a bad foundation, and thus he will have a bad outcome. What is left for the wicked that could turn out well, when what he considers good will turn out badly?

In what he places his greatest confidence are his sacrifices and the works he calls good, by which he thinks to discharge his evils and obligate God to give a prosperous outcome to all his affairs. As for sacrifices, it is already decreed that "the sacrifice of the wicked is an abomination to the LORD" (Proverbs 15), because all the works they do are without fulfillment and without the true fire of faith; they are without charity and without hope. Thus, works that are good in themselves are not lost or rejected because of themselves; but because of the hand that performs them. They are feigned before men, feigned before God, and feigned before the one who performs them: in short, they arise from a bad conscience and are not guided by the will of the Lord whom they claim to serve. It is rightly said that "the hope of the wicked will perish" (Job 8), because it is vain and without foundation.

Let the sinner seek whatever gains he wishes, surpass in the greed of his interests all the servants of the world; we will not contend with him on this, provided he does not deny that he does not do the works that the will of God demands, that he is not His servant nor vassal of His kingdom, that he has nothing with which to appear before His justice. If he wants to say he could be worse, perhaps he speaks the truth. If he wants God to reward him and give him heaven for not being worse, let him plead his case. If he is content because he moves among the dead, because in the eyes of the world he is green, because in comparison to others who are very wicked, he appears to be a tree that bears fruit, let him not deceive himself with the judgment of the world nor compare himself with those he considers much worse: let him see how he appears in the eyes of God, who is the true Judge and the Lord of the estate; let him measure himself against the righteous and hear the divine sentence which affirms that the good are like trees planted by streams of water, that bear their fruit in season, and whose leaves do not wither, and all they do prospers; while he is like dust so fine and of so little substance, that the wind carries it away from the face of the earth.

As is the tree, so is the fruit it bears (Matthew 7). It is eaten away from within by disobedience to God, by not fulfilling the purpose for which it was created, by lack of righteousness to appear in the presence of divine goodness, by contempt for His commandments, by audacity against His power, and sometimes, above all this, by the foolish confidence in what it does, by pride because it is not worse.

I seem to hear a familiar sound, a great discouragement for sinners, a great disheartenment for the wicked, asking how they can possibly reach heaven if this is true. It is impossible that such harsh sentences are as severe as they sound, nor that God is so displeased with them; and other things along this line. The previous sermon celebrated the favor of the righteous; today is the day of the disfavor of the wicked. The Divine Scripture is not partial, nor does it show favoritism. As the first was true, so is the second. Be frightened by what we have said, because your conscience knows it. Well, friend, if the sentence seems so harsh to you, abandon the guilt. If you do not want to be such bad dust, do not want to be such a bad man.

Consider that it is a great wickedness above all your wickedness to want to be so bad towards the Lord who created and redeemed you and waits for you; and that He should not be so just as to punish you and to honor His goodness. If you say you want to escape your misfortune, and you say it sincerely, then we will bring good news to you, because such news is given by the Divine Word. If you argue your inability, the misery of your strength, and the great power of your sin, you are doing well. The less you understand yourself capable of such a great thing, the more you recognize your weakness, the better you will succeed, and the more affectionately and confidently ask God for help for all of it, who will give it very fully.

Confess your misery and how little you can do, and there will be no lack of one who gives you such great strength and such great courage that all the power of the devil, which is the greatest on earth, will not suffice to resist you. Decide to ask, for He is ready to give; begin to seek your own good, for He has already begun to favor you; open your hands and heart, for He is inviting and urging you with what you need; strive to open your doors, for He is knocking at them; go out to meet Him, for He comes to seek you, and He waits only for you to go out.

But if you cite your weakness as an excuse to remain in your sins; if you confess the faintness of your strength to avoid taking advantage of God's strength; if you are a stubborn and rebellious sinner who wants to remain sleeping in the bed of your perdition, that neither the accusation of your own conscience, nor the great debt you owe to the Lord who created you, nor the threat of His Word, nor the fear of His judgment, can shake you from your evil slumber, then your blindness and pride are great in wanting to be pampered with all this, to hear sweet words, to be promised a good outcome on such a lost path, and for God to flatter His enemy, the one who despises His goodness and power, and to give him a kind of license to persist in such a wicked life.

If you consider it well, what such a sinner asks for is nothing other than what I just mentioned. He wants encouragement to continue further, hope to sustain him in his evil; it does not seem to him that his sin has a fully good taste unless it is accompanied by the pleasure of receiving good news or the assurance that, after fully indulging in the taste of his wickedness on earth, he will have a very prosperous outcome, suddenly finding himself in heaven. We cannot speak well of this evil lineage of men, as harshly speaks the One who knows them and will judge them.

What the end of the sinner will be, whether he will repent before he departs from this world; whether he will take advantage of the mercy that divine goodness offers him or not, we cannot know, nor should our curiosity dare to judge this secret. Only God knows, by whose clemency and powerful hand many who lived very wicked lives attained a most holy death. But as long as the sinner persists in his wickedness, as long as he despises the mercy of God that calls him and continues to add to or remain firm in the works of his sins, the Holy Scripture treats him harshly; it accuses and sentences him as an enemy of divine goodness; bad news is what it gives of him; great is the anger it shows against all his deeds; it predicts a wretched end for him: as is the path he takes, so it announces his destination.

And since this is the treatment that the Word of God gives him, it is sufficient proof that this is the medicine most suitable for his wounds; that with these cauterizations he must be cured, with such sentences they must attempt to break his hardness, with this weight they must value what he esteems, with this sound they must awaken him from that evil sleep and repose with which his wretched conscience attempts to sleep. And since this is what God does, says, and commands, this will be the most correct path, nor is it reasonable for me or anyone to attempt to deviate in another direction, or to treat such a sinner in any other way than the Lord Himself, who will be his Judge.

Be very attentive and consider if anything more severe can be said against the sinners we have spoken of, who are rebellious and obstinate, than what the Spirit of the Lord says today through our Prophet: "They are like the dust that the wind drives away from the face of the earth." Understand well and think about the nature and value of that dust, in relation and comparison to the trees planted by streams of water, of which we have already spoken, and you will see that nothing greater in disfavor of the wicked can be emphasized. This sentence is not alone in the Divine Scripture; all others that speak of this matter and with these circumstances echo this tone. There are no softer ones to appeal from one to the other.

You might think that God speaks in such places about a kind of sinners never seen in these parts; about men who lived in other times and lands; who had monstrous judgments and actions, very different from all others; who committed sins never heard of or thought about, who have already perished and left no memory. But you are greatly mistaken, for those whom the Divine Scripture thus threatens are more common and prevalent than you think. If you want to adhere to the truth, you have some reason. A sinner is indeed a monstrous thing, for he is so contrary to what God commands him to be, and like such an ugly and monstrous thing, he ought to be extremely rare in the world, seldom seen; all men ought to flee from him, and he from all others. But according to the judgment and manner in which these things are treated in the world, the truth is that these sinners of whom we speak are not as monstrous or frightful as you imagine.

They have faces like yours, and if you looked in a good mirror, you would find that they resemble you as closely as if they were your brothers or were you yourself. They know what you know, speak in the same manner, and understand the same things; even if you saw them at midnight, you would not flee or be startled by them, because there are such among this people, of such good appearance, that you would judge them to be saints and think they are on their way to heaven, so well dressed and shod. You have heard of their sins being mentioned, and you might even find them in the street, and perhaps in your own homes.

I am not one of the Stoics, who said that all sins were equal: I know well that some are more abominable and uglier than others; but for the monsters we speak of, the daily and commonly practiced evils are sufficient and even more than enough. To break God's commandments, in which He has declared His will, publicly shown His beauty and justice, and placed the threat of eternal hell for those who despise them, does it not seem to you that this is enough for such sinners to be understood as what the Divine Scripture says? Does it not seem enough for one to be greedy, a thief, a deceiver of his neighbor, a perjurer, a fornicator, a bearer of false witness, a murderer in hands or heart, scandalous and a bad example, a hindrance to the glory of God, a despiser of His mercy and justice—does it not seem enough for such people to be said to be like dust that the wind drives away from the face of the earth?

Must they necessarily be Pharaohs, Sardanapalus, and Judas; must they necessarily be worse than beasts for God to be angry with them and for His word to treat them with wrath? Especially since these individuals have the stubbornness and persistence we have mentioned, being so settled in their wickedness, with such neglect of what they should do, and so much care to continue in the evil they do. Against these, divine justice shows itself so rigorous, whereas, for the others, we have already discussed how the same Scripture gives us good hope.

Christian charity and the greatness of the mercy and goodness of the Lord invite and obligate us all to trust that He will extend His powerful hand over any sinner, no matter how abominable and cursed they may seem to us. But we also know that if a person is so rebellious that they refuse to take advantage of what the supreme goodness does for them, in the end, what the justice of the same Lord has ordained against those who despise it will be executed upon them. Despite this, the blindness of many sinners is such that they fail to understand that such harsh things are said about them; they always insist that their sins are not so great that they should be treated in this way; they imagine that there are greater evils than breaking the commandments of God.

I have already stated that some sins are greater than others, and I have also said that transgressing the commandments we all know by heart, in the manner I have described, is sufficient cause for all those who find such pleasure in their sins that they wish to persist in them to take these threats upon themselves. I thought there was only one kind of perfection, that of those who not only keep the commandments but also observe the counsels. They say that if they do not want to be perfect, no one obliges them; they can leave the counsels and take the commandments. But it also seems to me that another kind of perfection is practiced, and if not in word, at least in deed.

You will find people who consider themselves Christian without keeping the commandments, at least not as they should be kept. It must seem to them that this too is a counsel; that it is within their freedom to take it or leave it; that keeping the commandments in the way that is required is a matter of great sanctity, meaning excessive perfection, which is for the very advanced and spiritual; for those who do not want to be so holy, but only to enter heaven, other sanctities, other devotions, and things with which they canonize themselves suffice; with which it seems to them that they can pass and live as they please. This is not discussed as clearly as I say it, but it is put into practice as clearly as I say it. Who do you think are those for whom this digression began, whose voices I seemed to hear, complaining that we narrow the path too much for them, that we close all the doors, that we despair them with the threats of Holy Scripture? None other than these; because those who clearly recognize and take for themselves what God says do not say this. For we demand nothing but the keeping and fulfillment of the commandments. We do not ask people to forcibly become monks, nor to go sleep in caves, much less to perform miracles or speak with angels. You must keep the ten commandments, man, if you do not want to be an enemy of God.

This admonition, which you now laugh at as something you learned with your mother's milk, is the one that scandalizes you, the one you find so harsh and strong and such a hard obligation; this is the sentence you appeal from and the yoke your conscience so much struggles to cast off. You do not say that you find the commandments of God disagreeable, for you abhor such blasphemy; but you wish they were less stringent, allowing you the pride of your vanity, revenge against your neighbor, little fear of God, deceit in your dealings; that holy water would wash away your looseness and impurities; that you would not be required to suffer the cross, wage war against yourself, or practice true mortification.

And since the commandments demand this, you do not wish, or rather, you do not dare to complain about them; but about me or others in my office, for not diluting them so that they do not cut so deeply into your heart. But it would be good to account for this so that you may see how much sin blinds those whom the world considers wise, and how aptly it is said that carnal prudence is very vain and foolish when it comes to the things of God, and how great a folly the things of God seem when examined by human wisdom (Romans 8; 1 Corinthians 2).

Tell me, friend, if you think it a severe sentence that, if you are a sinner and wicked, you should be like dust driven away by the wind from the face of the earth, what is it that you find so objectionable? Perhaps it is said in obscure words, and in place of one, we put another? It is very clear and much clearer if you take advantage of the comparison in the preceding verse, where it is said that the righteous are like a tree planted by streams of water, etc. So, who do you complain about: God or me? You would not dare to say the former, although I understand you well. Of me, for what? Because I emphasize these words, do not soften them, do not mix them in such a way that they do not hurt you so much and leave you more at peace, with more tranquility and hope? Have I guessed correctly? I think so.

I do not want to tell you now how treacherous I would be to you in that; I will take another path. Suppose I were as good in your opinion, and as bad in mine, as to do what you want, tell me honestly: would you believe me? Do you not see that God is on one side and I on the other? He says that you are the finest dust and of the least substance imaginable; I, to please you or out of my vanity, would go to the ends of the earth to make you believe that at least you are something, and would you believe me? How can I lessen the emphasis? Do you not see what was said of the righteous: a fruitful tree, full of leaves, that everything it does prospers? Well, take the opposite and see what you are; and you must accept it because the other is a friend of God and you are an enemy.

What am I to do here? God cures you by cauterization, and am I to cure you with balm? He speaks in the fullness of His wisdom and has sworn that in all His Scripture and His law there is not a jot that is not true and must be fulfilled (Matthew 5), and you want me to affirm that He is mocking you and that His Word is not entirely true? If you want to see clearly, this is what you ask of me, although you would swear otherwise. But in this, you are not to be believed because you are so deceived that you give me such great authority in this matter and so much credit that you would believe my roundabout ways and vanities in glossing things to your liking more than the clarity and simplicity of the Divine Word, which so fully says that you are like dust driven by the wind from the face of the earth. Outside of this, you would not give me the authority to judge whether snow is cold; and you are so blind and deceived in this that you are on the path to believing me more than God. And to show you that I speak the truth, you are a witness that you are prepared to give me more credit than your own conscience if I were to tell you what you want to hear.

This has been said so that, since we are discussing and must continue to discuss in the remainder of our sermon the threats of divine justice against the sinner, it is clear that the sinner has no one to blame but himself, unless he wants to complain about God. He must endure being treated in such a manner and be certain that no exaggeration of any misery or lack of goods can compare with the great evil of being an enemy of such a Lord and wanting to persist in enmity.

Returning to our purpose, we were discussing how the sinner is reduced to dust and so devoid of virtue, so lacking in the roots of true faith, true charity, and true hope, that he has neither fruit nor semblance of a tree for God, his neighbor, or himself; instead, he is like dust raised and scattered by the wind. In the same comparison, as you have already heard, all this is emphasized, for in such fine dust, as our Prophet indicates, there is no root, no moisture, no fruit, no leaf, no resistance to prevent the wind from carrying it away and scattering it where there will never again be a sign or memory of it. Finally, everything is contrary, as we have already said, to what is stated in the other verse about the just man, who is like a tree whose every product prospers.

There is another subtlety in the comparison, which further elucidates what has been discussed and places the sinner in greater distress. For trees, summer is the most suitable time. When the heat is most intense, they are at their most beautiful, with fresher leaves and the best season for fruit. For the chaff and straw of the ears of wheat, everything happens contrariwise; for when the wheat reaches maturity, they dry up, are threshed and trampled, and turned into such light dust that any wind can carry it away. Thus, the driest and hottest time is the season of greatest prosperity for most trees, and this same time reveals how flimsy the greenery of the straw of the ears of wheat was, and within a few days, it is treated in such a way that it is turned into dust with which all winds play.

Divine Providence ordered that the part of the year in which it seems to us that nothing green should remain is the most suitable season for the vast majority of the world's trees, in which they show the most beautiful fruits and leaves, manifesting in this the great care He has for us, and putting such order in everything with His wisdom, that they themselves call us to understand that our goods and favors depend solely on Him, and that if we place our hope in Him, there is no time or adversity that can take it away. I have brought this up so that you may see how the same analogy used in the Psalm reveals the disaster of the wicked from all angles. When others have the summer of their fruition, and all the dryness in the world is not enough to prevent it, rather it seems to help them, then sinners have the winter of their perdition and the end of that beautiful color they once showed.

We began to discuss the sacrifices and good deeds of the wicked and the obstinate in their wickedness, which gave occasion for such lengthy digressions, although not entirely without purpose. Now it is fitting to continue what we had begun, to see if these threats, which the sinner calls discouragements, will dishearten him enough to make some effort to leave such a bad life. If you carefully consider what is the summer of the wicked we are talking about, you will find no other than the one he himself chooses and confesses.

This consists of his good works and sacrifices. His good work, as you already heard, on one hand, means: not being worse. If he sometimes takes your coat, he graciously leaves you your shirt; if he tramples you and kicks you, he does not finish you off; if he says much ill of you, he does not bear false witness against you before the judge; if he is an adulterer, he is not a thief; if he is a thief, he is not a murderer; if he is a murderer, he does not blaspheme; if he blasphemes, he is not a traitor; if he takes your wife, he leaves you your daughter; and in this way, you can continue at length along the path of his good works. "Well, let's see, isn't it worse to be worse?" I do not deny that. If you pretend nothing else and are content with that, we will clearly confess that it is much worse and more abominable and farther from God to have all the faults we have mentioned than to have half of them. If you are satisfied that you are not the worst nor among the worst, you may be right, and we will not argue about that. What I began to say is that the good works of such wicked people mean not being worse, and they themselves confess it. I say further that, on the other hand, their good works mean that, after having blasphemed, they crossed themselves with almost as much anger as when they blasphemed.

I want to go further and admit that there are many of these wicked sinners of whom we speak, who are generous to others, who are very abstemious and lead a very orderly life; and to be brief, I say that sometimes they have many things we call moral virtues and things of religion, and they also have their prayers and attend mass, and we could continue further. "Well, do you call these bad works?" We are not discussing the works here, but you; I do not say that the works are bad, but that you are bad, and that they do not excuse you from being dust carried away by the wind if you are among the sinners we have described. Are you satisfied? I say then that these works, as good as they may be in themselves, lose so much by being in your hands that when, proud of them, you think that the summer of your fruition has arrived and that you are like other trees, then is your true winter, and in truth, you are like dust carried away by the wind from the face of the earth.

What do you think the fruit is, and the branches, and the leaves of the chaff that swirl in the wind? That is yours. If this, with which you are so proud, so confident, and foolish, is not the dust carried away by the wind, what do you think the verse of our Psalm refers to? The evil deeds, which in themselves are works of the devil, are carried away by a thousand winds. They never had any greenery, neither true nor false, neither in the eyes of the good nor in the eyes of the bad. Haven't I already told you that the end of our verse is the opposite of the end we explained in the previous sermon?

All things of the righteous prosper there. I return to say that you take the opposite of that, and in all clarity, the things of the wicked have adversity. The others were so good, they abhorred their evil deeds so much that, if by chance they fell into them, they derived profit from their sins, not because there is any good in sin, but because such is the craftsmanship of God's mercy; you are so wicked for loving your evils so much, for being so hardened in them, that the works that are good in themselves lose their value in you. If you are content with less value than pleasing God and think you are very rich while still being His enemy and condemned to be dust in the presence of His great wrath, value them as you will, and sell them to whomever you please, for on that point, I have already told you that we will never have a dispute.

Provided you do not deny what the Lord says about such works performed by sinners and friends of their sin, rejoice in whatever else you may claim and keep it safe if you can. Great is the misfortune that stems from your rebellion regarding your good works, for this reason they do not yield full fruit. You would be worse if you did not perform them; you remain more of an enemy of God. Without such good fruit, I do not know why you are so content with the others you wish to bear. This is the reason why all of this is so poorly treated in the Sacred Scripture, because the sinner defrauds what the works were supposed to achieve, and seeks the false and the little, losing the much and the true. What does God say about the sacrifices of the wicked? "To what purpose is this incense from Sheba to me, and the sweet cane from a far country? Your burnt offerings are not acceptable, nor are your sacrifices pleasing to me" (Jeremiah 6). The reason for the Lord's discontent with such works is not in the law He ordained, for the law is truly holy, and the commandment is holy, and just, and good (Romans 7). It is not in the sacrifices themselves, which are works of His law, with which He intended to be served and honored among men.

On the other hand, the disdain for these works arises from nothing other than the wickedness of the sinner's heart, the falsehood with which they are offered, and the foolish confidence placed in them to take more rest and more pleasure in their sin; for on one hand, he says he does not want to leave it, and on the other, he wants to have the Lord pleased for the time it suits him.

Nothing can bring us into as much awareness of how great the wickedness of these sinners is, who are so fond of their sins and so persevering in them, as this very point we are discussing, that the purity of good works falls apart in their hands, so that the Lord does not accept them as something from His servants, but rather says He abhors them. "To the pure all things are pure, but to those who are defiled and unbelieving nothing is pure; even their mind and conscience are defiled" (Titus 1). Perhaps the wicked think they are bearing fruit through prayer and thus consider themselves trees, but it is worth noting how they think God should hear them, while they do not hear His commandments. "One who turns away his ear from hearing the law, even his prayer is an abomination" (Proverbs 28). If, with anguish from the evil caused by his sin, he asks for remedy, let him hasten to leave it and benefit from his prayer; but if he wishes to remain at ease in his wickedness, fearing the yoke of Christ because it seems too heavy and the devil's yoke seems very light, let us refer to him to count the benefits he thinks he gains from his prayer, since he does not want to believe in the Divine Scripture regarding this matter.

I could continue at greater length, convincing the sinner that all the threats pronounced by the Word of God against him are true, and clarifying the value of the things we have said; but it seems appropriate to leave it for the following sermon, where it will be as fitting a place as this, in which, with the Lord's favor, we will respond to everything he might argue, if he still believes in his judgment that he has something to argue, and extend more fully on this very matter. At present, nothing remains but to recall the infidelity and misery that the Holy Spirit, through the prophet David, says the wicked possess, for while the righteous are trees of such beauty as we have described, from which nothing comes that is not prosperous, the sinners are such powerless and useless dust that the wind carries away and sweeps from the face of the earth.

Indeed, it says, "from the face of the earth," because they have no roots in it, though they strive much to be rooted in it. Their faith is full of distrust; their love for God is to disobey

Him, their love for men is for their own interests and carnal desires; their hope is in vain dreams; their remedies and medicines are without virtue and efficacy. Where there are no true roots, there can be no true fruits. Let him reflect on what love for God there can be in one who daily disrespects Him, what charity there can be where there is no God, what hope can exist that is not strengthened by His word. If all this does not instill fear, does not shock or awaken him from such an evil and deep slumber, let him continue his misfortune, for one day he will see the truth; but if this frightens and startles him, as it should and as the very Word of God seeks and intends, let him immediately put his hands to the task, ask the Lord for remedy and take it, and, like a man seeking his own life in a forest of such thickness and dangers as night approaches, let him not tire or rest until he finds it.

Let him strive to produce not false, but true fruits of repentance, for God is powerful to make dust a most fertile soil, and to plant those of no substance and give them deep roots and raise them into most beautiful trees whose fruit delights the angels and even the Lord Himself. The divine power has not diminished, nor has His goodness narrowed, so that He cannot now do what He promised so many years ago to the idolatrous and lost nations, affirming with His Word that the desert and the solitary place shall be glad for them; that the wilderness shall rejoice and blossom as the rose; that He will pour water upon him that is thirsty, and floods upon the dry ground (Isaiah 35 and 44).

God is a great teacher, capable of re-grafting the cut and dry branches, and making them fruitful again. Let the sinner humble himself and, if only out of fear of the wrath that the Lord so powerfully displays against him, and with such just reason to be angry, begin to seek remedy. Let him strive to know himself and to know Him who is waiting for him, so that he may fear Him rightly, and justly love Him. Let him forget his foolish confidences and stop believing in his vain dreams. Let him see that from lost paths there can be no good news, and that the more he walks them, the more certain are the dangers of arriving at a bad destination. If repentance seems harsh, let him understand that when God has promised a good end, the toil of the journey is to be considered lightly. If the medicine is bitter, such is required by the disease. He who seeks will not be hidden from him, nor will they who have offered be denied; he has a guide who will go with him, giving him health for his sickness, they will heal him so that, bearing good fruit, what was dead will be resurrected, so that he may live and attain afterward an eternal and great reward.

The Fifth Sermon

*Por tanto, no se levantarán en el juicio los malos,
los pecadores en la congregación de los justos.*[12]

THIS VERSE contains a sentence worthy of great weight and consideration, and one of much dread for the wicked. It follows logically from what we discussed in the preceding verse and provides the reason for the judgment of sinners, concerning what happens to them in this world and what will happen to them after they leave it. We explained how the wicked are like dust carried away by the wind; now it adds and says that from this, it follows that they will not stand in the judgment nor in the congregation of the righteous, referring also to what was said about sinners: that some are like well-planted and watered trees, and that everything they do prospers, while others are like chaff and dust carried by the wind.

To make all this clearer, it is good to first explain the terms, and then proceed to declare how it follows from the previous points. The first term here is "stand," because it says that the wicked will not stand in the judgment. To stand here means as much as to resist or to remain firm. This meaning that I have mentioned is very common in the Divine Scripture, as it is a metaphor taken from the principal and primary meaning. He who stands is firm to resist and remain. The children of Israel could not stand before their enemies, instead they turned their

---

12. "Therefore the wicked will not stand in the judgment, nor sinners in the congregation of the righteous;" (Ps. 1:5, ESV)

backs before their enemies, said God to Joshua (7). It is the same term in this sentence and in our verse: in both parts, it is to stand; it means they will not be able to remain standing against them. There are many places in Scripture where this can be proven, which I refrain from bringing here because it is unnecessary. In the Spanish language, this manner of speaking is also very common; as one resists another, we say "he stood against him." Bringing it to our purpose, our verse means that the wicked cannot stand, cannot remain, nor have firmness in the judgment, nor sinners in the company and congregation of the righteous.

It remains to explain what is meant by this term "judgment," so that we have a complete understanding of our verse. Judgment here means the account that God takes of men when He visits them, when He reasons with them, when He upholds His justice and manifests His wrath against the wicked, and His favor towards the righteous. In this judgment, our Prophet says, the wicked do not remain, nor do they stay in the congregation of the righteous. The reason is that the wicked are like dust that the wind carries and scatters. In this, as I said, it gives a much greater explanation of the two preceding verses and makes an allusion or a point to the two comparisons: of the righteous being like trees, and of the sinners being like dust; the trees remain firm, the dust is carried away from among them.

It also makes us understand in these words the difference between God's judgment and the world's judgment; between the account He makes and the account men make. In the judgment of the world, as we said in the previous sermon, often sinners appear as very beautiful trees, very well planted, with many leaves and much fruit; and from this, they are coveted and highly esteemed. On the contrary, the righteous appear as stubble, as dust, with no one to water them, no one to take care of them, no one to defend them or expect fruit from them. But when God takes the account, when He makes an investigation and judgment of these matters, the deception is immediately discarded; the wicked are carried away like the dust they were, and the righteous remain alone and firm like well-planted trees. And if both the righteous and the wicked seemed like trees, and the judgment and justice of men regarded them as equally friends and favored by God, this deception is also undone, the trees remain, and the dust disappears. Therefore, God's judgment is here compared to a spirit of great impetus and tempest, which carries away everything before it that is not well planted and does not have great firmness. So it is compared in another part by our Prophet: "Pursue them with your tempest, O Lord, and terrify them with your whirlwind" (Psalm 83). And this is a very frequent comparison in Sacred Scripture.

Now, it is appropriate to discuss this judgment and explain, as far as possible, the manner in which the wicked are dispersed and the righteous remain. There are three judgments of God towards men, that is, three ways in which He examines them through the justice of His Word, regarding how they serve or do not serve Him. In all three judgments, it is true to say that the righteous have resistance, and like trees with good roots, they remain firm, while the wicked are sifted out and carried away powerfully like dust among the trees in a tempest.

The primary judgment mentioned in Scripture is the final one, in which Christ, our Redeemer, Lord, and Judge of men, will take the ultimate account of what each person did, said, and thought, with such a delicate examination that even idle words will come under scrutiny for how time was spent on them. In this judgment, everything our Psalm says will occur; the good and the wicked will be separated from one another, just as the good shepherd separates the goats from the sheep (Matthew 25). Before this separation, the flock moves together, and it is difficult to discern which is a sheep and which is a goat: the complete knowledge of this is reserved for the great Shepherd. That judgment is rigorous, but in the end, the righteous stand firm in it, and like strong, well-rooted trees, they remain in perpetual friendship with God, heirs of the kingdom of heaven forever.

The wicked try to resist, and though they are like chaff and dust, they attempt to defend themselves as if they were trees: "Lord, when did we see you hungry, or thirsty, or naked, or sick, or in prison, and did not serve you?" But in the end, they are met with that sentence and carried away: "Depart from me, you accursed, into the eternal fire prepared for the devil and his angels." As it is said by Saint Luke (3) of Christ, our Redeemer: "His winnowing fork is in his hand, to clear his threshing floor and to gather the wheat into his barn, but the chaff he will burn with unquenchable fire." I do not want to dwell longer on this judgment, as you have heard of it many times; may God allow it to benefit you. For our purpose, it suffices to say that, in speaking of it, what our Psalm says is true: the wicked do not stand in it, nor do they remain in the congregation of the righteous.

Let us speak of the other two judgments, which are no less mentioned in Scripture and which you ought to have complete knowledge of if you wish to understand yourselves and what God wants. I say that the second judgment occurs whenever, through His Word, the Lord takes account of man, scrutinizes his heart, and makes a judgment within his conscience through its testimony. Of this judgment, it is also true to say that it casts down the wicked, just as we affirmed that dust is carried away, and it leaves the righteous firm, separated from that bad company, like well-planted trees. It is good to explain this because it is very necessary; and the worse it may seem to the sinner, the more certain a sign it is that the medicine would be more beneficial if he would accept it.

I have often said that every wicked person who, persisting in their wickedness and taking pleasure in it, thinks they will be saved and bring a prosperous end to all their matters, is, in a certain sense, a hypocrite, because all their deeds are deceit and delusion, a feigned dawn before God and themselves. Such a person persuades themselves that they are a tree, that they have roots, leaves, and fruit; they do not fully understand that they are the dust we have discussed. This imagination lasts for a time, God permits it, and their sin deceives them so that they walk in this delusion and foolish contentment. But when the Divine Word comes and the Lord sends it through the hand of a true minister sent by Him, and when it is embedded in the heart of such a sinner, then they truly enter into judgment, it becomes clear how they were a feigned tree, and it is clearly seen how they do not stand; on the contrary, the righteous remain lifted and firm in that same judgment.

Let us explain both: how the wicked do not stand and how the righteous remain. Sinners have a wavering conscience; they never remain in a stable state. They are dealt with in various ways; like something without roots that cannot remain firm, sometimes they are confident, and other times greatly disheartened, without more reason than the various judgments of their own conscience. One day they think God does not understand them, according to what Isaiah says: "Who sees us and who knows us?" To which God responds: "Your subversion will indeed be regarded as the potter's clay. Shall the work say of him who made it, 'He did not make me'? Or shall the thing formed say of him who formed it, 'He has no understanding'?" (Isaiah 29). Then comes the delusion of their madness, the waves of their rest and pleasure; the Lord lets them imagine they are in darkness, so hidden that their deeds cannot be understood. After this time, another comes when the same wicked lose all that vain joy they had previously dreamed of. Thus they say through Jeremiah: "It is useless, for we will walk after our own devices, and we will that all do the imagination of his evil heart" (Jeremiah 18). They speak like people who, entering into account with God, see no remedy if they are to be guided that way, showing how much disquiet the Word of the Lord places in the obstinate sinner's heart when it enters with rigorous judgment of what must be done if they do not want to be lost.

The reason for this variety is that the wicked have a very great love and affection for their sin. From this same affection arises sometimes this madness and boldness of security with which they find themselves so well, and they promise themselves the same end and outcome of all their matters with much contentment. From this same affection comes at other times the fear of losing what they covet. Hence their shocks and disquiet, fearing to be understood and treated as they are. "The wicked flee when no one pursues," says Solomon (Proverbs 28). "The wicked are like the troubled sea, which cannot rest, whose waters cast up mire and dirt" (Isaiah 57).

This vacillation and unrest go much further in the consciences and hearts of these great sinners. The carelessness in which the wicked live when they sleep in their iniquities, that security with which they proceed so far, that weaving of such a long web, and building so in their own perdition as if it were never to be undone, that drinking of what tastes good to them as if it would never taste bad, is nothing but a pretense that there is neither God (Psalm 52) nor hell, nor will they be judged as the Gospel says. This pretense is so secret, so hidden in the dens of their wickedness, that they themselves would swear they do not have it; it is easier to prove that they are not without it.

On the other hand, when the wicked person is prompted by religion and acknowledges that God exists, that His Word is true, that there will be a judgment of the good and the bad, that there are rewards for some and punishment for others, even then they often strive to maintain, and do maintain, their false security. They confess that there is God's law, but they craft it to suit their own needs, shaping and cutting it as they see fit. If such a person truly understood themselves, they would realize that they are the author of that law, for they interpret it, measure it, and make it narrow or broad according to the folly of their mind.

After this comes God's judgment, when His Word is taught by His true ministers with the same value and force that He intends. As soon as the Word performs its duty, you will see turmoil in the heart of the wicked; they try to resist and cannot, all of which is clearly shown by the sadness, the offense, and scandal they experience, by their avoidance of care, by their desire to distance the Word from themselves, by their regret of having heard it, by their attempt to divert it elsewhere, as conjurers do with storms. In this way, Amaziah said that the land could not bear Amos's preaching (Amos 7). Thus, the wicked are overthrown by the Word, and this is why they are scandalized, because they see themselves falling and have no branches to hold on to. This is the judgment and power of Christ through His Word and ministers, according to what is said by Isaiah (11): "With the breath of his lips, he will slay the wicked."

We have explained how, as long as the wicked manage their affairs with their own judgment, it seems to go well for them; but when God's judgment enters the heart, they are immediately defeated and overthrown by their own fear, and that fear is the work of God's judgment and the punishment of His hand; a testimony to the law that the sinner breaks, a prediction of the condemnation they await for daring to oppose the powerful hand of their Creator who has done so much for them. Thus, He says in Deuteronomy (28): "The Lord will give you a trembling heart, failing eyes, and a despairing soul." This must accompany the conscience of the wicked who persist in their wickedness, the moment they are convicted by God's judgment through the power of His Word.

You will understand all this more clearly through an example, and let it be that of Cain, who is a prototype of the condition of sinners and what God's judgment works in them. Cain, although he had killed his brother, still had confidence in his sacrifices and walked securely, thinking he would not be lost, vainly confident, deceiving himself and deceiving God. When the Lord begins to call him to account, he responds shamelessly: "Am I my brother's keeper?" (Genesis 4). These words clearly reveal the false and vain confidence with which he walked securely. But as God's judgment presses and goes further, tightening the account and making him understand that he is understood, he immediately falls into despair.

I have already said that the first thing, which is to try to hide from God, is a characteristic of the wicked, as they themselves testify or, rather, as the Divine Word makes them testify, as manifested in Psalm 94: "The LORD does not see; the God of Jacob takes no notice." Some may say that no one is so foolish as to think they can hide their heart from God. To this, I say that there are many fools touched by this madness, which is easy to prove, and if you were attentive, we have already proven it a little when we spoke of the offense and scandal they receive when God's Word demands from them what is not convenient for their purpose, nor aligns with their interests; when it undoes the vanity of their foolish penances, when it requires true works and purity of heart. They do not understand this madness, it is true; but God understands it, for He affirms that they have it. Consider among good men: to whom should we give more credit: what the Divine Scripture says about the sinner, or what the sinner says about himself?

There is no need to argue much about this, as we have very clear evidence to refute these vanities in two actions of sinners: one is when they are convinced and repent; the other is when they are convinced and do not repent. The wicked person who, at some point, rested in their sinful life, trying to mitigate their sin for themselves, flattering their own deeds, making up for their sins with satisfactions they deemed sufficient, being the evaluator and judge of their own affairs and the outcome they expected, and later came to a true understanding, realized their perdition and how mistaken their account was, renounced all their foolishness, truly subjected themselves to God's will; desiring certain mortification with great suffering to fulfill it, such a person is well-suited to be a judge of what we say. Let them speak and confess if it is true that they had such madness in their heart, which they did not recognize until they were overthrown and convicted in God's judgment.

An example of this sinner we have described is our prophet David, who understood so much more about himself in an instant when he found himself sentenced in God's judgment, than he had in many days when he neglected his sin, not considering himself as lost as he later found himself. He exclaims in Psalm 19: "Who can understand man's errors? Cleanse me from secret faults." What must be the things that other great sinners do not understand, who never afflicted themselves as he did, not even with many leagues?

Of the other sinners, we already gave the example of Cain, who, although convicted of his sin, did not want to do penance. Even so, it is well understood from him the madness and folly with which he had first sustained himself. He confesses the greatness of his wickedness, remains full of fear, flees from the presence of God, and fears that everyone who finds him will kill him. All of this is nothing but the effects of the knowledge of his wickedness.

One might ask this fool what novelty there was then compared to before, that at one time he fled so full of fears and alarms, and at another, he was so carefree, secure, and confident. He could not respond that he did not know it was a great wickedness to kill his own brother, and to kill him out of envy and betrayal, and to kill an innocent. He spoke with God and initially was as daring as if he had a good case. So what is this that happens? What is this great change? It is because God's judgment completed its work in him, revealed his madness, and uncovered his wickedness. Cain had knowledge of his sin, but he did not have knowledge of divine mercy. If he had understood the latter as he understood the former, he would have been freed.

Whether sinners wish it or not, they must come to know their sin. Woe to those who delay this recognition, only to face despair, as we know will happen to the wicked on the Day of Judgment! How much better it is not to flee from self-understanding! For, no matter how many evils we acknowledge in ourselves, the clemency and gentleness of the Judge, who desires our self-awareness to prevent our perdition, is greater. Now, whether in one way or another, we have proven that the sinner is overthrown in God's judgment, carried away like dust, without resistance, unless they choose to undergo a transformation as great and marvelous as if a piece of chaff, incapable of being ground, were to be transformed into a great, beautiful tree full of fruit.

In the previous sermon, if you recall, we began discussing this same subject, as all these matters are intertwined, with one statement leading to another because they are interdependent. We promised that in this verse we would conclude the folly and vanity with which sinners fail to understand they are dust, by opposing many other things that they believe are sufficient to rescue them from this danger. No one is as proud of the good they do as a sinner. The price of their good deed cannot be estimated if we go by their valuation. They not only sell it dearly to men, but they also sell it so dearly to God that they use it as an excuse and counterweight for the sins they love and harbor in their hearts.

We have already said that regardless of how the wicked imagine the value of their deeds, and in whatever way they wish to use them to their advantage, the conclusion remains that they are not sufficient to excuse them from being the dust carried away by the wind. For this same reason, all these things are of such weak and vain resistance in the judgment of conscience when God judges in it, that they will not prevent them from being overthrown and disappeared in the same judgment, and completely separated from the congregation of the just. And because the instrument by which this judgment is made is the true Word of God, which is living and powerful, and sharper than any two-edged sword; and discerns the thoughts and intentions of the hearts, both of the good and the bad (Hebrews 4), and it is the prosecutor of all these causes, it is only right that we use it to leave the presumption of sinners without a response.

Let us now speak to such individuals. Come here, lost man, who is so far from the satisfaction of your sin, and thinks you will traverse this entire journey with the help of God, as you say. How do you sleep so securely in the meantime? What does your conscience respond to its own accusation and to the accusation the Lord places in it through His Word? "My good works, my prayers, and my sacrifices respond: if I did not have these, do not consider me so foolish as to sleep securely. If I were like other wicked people who do not have these my merits, I would not rest at all." And do you believe that you stand firm in God's judgment where your own conscience is a witness? Oh traitor, how you deceive yourself! Let us understand: By what means do you think that God values your deeds so much that they are enough for you to remain in His judgment when He, through your own conscience, accuses you of your wickedness and your persistence in such a bad state? There is no way but that you presume on the necessity you imagine He has for your services, or on the deception you think you can accomplish, selling Him lead for gold. If you find another basis for your confidence, bring it to light, if you dare, for I stake my head that it will be more vain than these two.

To address the first point, let us consider how much God needs the goods of the righteous, and by this measure, we can judge how much He needs the goods of the wicked. We need not turn to any other witness but our own Prophet. "You have said, O my soul, to the LORD, 'You are my Lord; my goodness does not extend to You'" (Psalm 16). If the most compelling thing for a saint to magnify is the greatness of the divine, and understands how fitting it is to dedicate oneself entirely to His service realizing that He is such a rich and powerful Lord that He neither has nor can have any need of others' goods, then where do the services of the wicked stand, or what lack does He have of them? Who gave you goods, man, that you think God could need them? If you are rich, it is by His hand; and if you are poor, it is your fault because you are so lacking that you don't even want to receive what is offered, and you want to compete with Him over who has more?

If we consider it carefully, the thought that the Lord must be content with your wicked goods out of a need for them is nothing but the great folly of dreaming that you have more than He does. The justified sinner would now mock his own deeds, and he would mock me and the vain imagination by which I condemn him; because he is not so foolish, nor of such mad thoughts, as to imagine that God can be hungry for him to feed, or in debt for him to lend money, or other such things. These vanities are mine, not his. So be it, that he is not so foolish, but we will prove that he is much more foolish: he cannot deny the pride of what he claims to do well; for if this did not reside in his heart, the dispute we are having would be superfluous, and it is only his obstinacy, his refusal to humble himself, his flight from confessing that he is dust, and his pertinacity in his own defense that prevents the judgment of God within his own conscience from overthrowing him. If he were to surrender and openly confess his misery, it would greatly benefit him and spare us the labor of tormenting him and dissecting his follies.

Now that it is conceded that his good deeds make him proud, let us declare just one thing: on what is that pride founded? He will argue that it is not pride, and may God forbid it should be. So be it: let us say it is confidence or hope if he prefers; let us call the black Juan white, let us give him this contentment, which will not last long. That hope, my friend, who sustains it? That candle with which you light yourself, on what wax or what oil does it burn? Why is God content with your goods, in the manner you think? Not because He needs them for eating or spending; we have agreed on this. Another need must remain hidden in your imagination, that of being honored, being respected, being served by you. It seems to you that He takes it as a form of hunger, and that in such a great multitude of wicked, and extremely wicked, people, He does not take it halfway; but values greatly that you make a reverence, and show in the world that you consider Him your Lord.

You are not the first to have fallen into these follies; it is an old delusion and no more valuable for it. By the path on which you are lost, those who said, "The temple of the LORD, the temple of the LORD are these" (Jeremiah 7) also walked and were lost. They thought that because there was no other temple in the whole earth dedicated to the name of the true Lord, except that in which they entered and worshiped and made sacrifices, God, as needing this honor, would forgive them everything else and not allow them to be punished according to the words of the prophets.

We have encountered your folly in the actions of your neighbors. And to show you that this is no less than the other folly you mocked, I tell you truly that God has as little need of your service for His honor as He has of your wealth for His sustenance. Diminishing and dishonoring His greatness in the first respect is no less than in the second. I would very much like you to understand how secure the Lord's glory and honor are. To desire to be served and glorified by you is a great favor He bestows upon you, revealing to you the means by which you can gain more. It is something due to who He is and a great mercy towards mankind.

The arrangement by which this is guided is that He formed you to reflect His likeness; so that from the works of your hands, the knowledge of who your Maker is would arise. This is part of the image spoken of in Scripture when it says God formed man in His image and likeness (Genesis 1). This is the path by which the works of the righteous are so acceptable because they correspond to their proper end and originate from the image and representation of the Lord, which is preserved in the souls of the good as the root and true foundation of true goodness, guiding us by divine mercy to receive great favors from the hand of whom we serve.

In all other respects, God has little need for our goods or services. His honor is so secure that there is no power in the world that can take it from Him or hinder it. You should consider what you want to choose: whether you want to give Him honor and glory through the path of His mercy and your benefit, or else you will give it to Him, though unwillingly, through the path of His justice and your harm. Do not fear that His glory will leave His house, because whatever you take from Him in one way, you will have to give back in another. Nor should you think that you can deceive Him by offering false things as true, no matter how much you strive; because when you strive to deceive yourself, you end up trying to deceive Him. You are sorely mistaken, and if you want to know, listen to what He says through our Prophet: "You thought, traitor, and you have pretended in your heart, that we are all alike, and that I am like you. You hypocrite, that is to say, you liar and vain person, you deceiver and self-deceived, did you think that I would truly be like you? You are on a bad path, I will enter into judgment with you and bring your iniquities to light, making you such a sure witness against yourself that you will have nothing to say, revealing who you are and what you attempted to be" (Psalm 50).

This, I believe, suffices to convince the wicked of their vain confidences when they reassure and delude themselves, becoming even more foolish than before by the works of their hands. Their follies are no less when they rise and show pride through their petitions and prayers, which is well worth proving here, as we have already begun and promised elsewhere. Answer now, do you feel content with yourselves? What prayer do you recite? If you recite the Lord's Prayer as the Redeemer of the world taught and commanded us, we have you in our grasp. What is it you say? "Our Father who art in heaven, hallowed be Thy name." Are you mocking Him, or do you mean it sincerely? Do you truly desire what you ask for, or is it merely perfunctory? If it is the latter, then you seek to deceive Him, proving our point even more than we desired. If it is the former, how is it possible that you truly desire the honor and glory of God and the obedience to His commandments, yet act so contrarily? Why do you not act upon it if it comes from your heart? Or do you confess clearly: "Lord, I say this for others, not for myself; let others sanctify You while I dishonor You."

Let's go further. "Thy kingdom come." Explain what you mean; if not, I will interpret it for you, if you trust me. "Thy kingdom come, but when it comes, I will flee so as not to enter; because if I wanted to enter, it is already here for me." What do you say next? "Thy will be done on earth as it is in heaven." Look at what this man desires and compare his words to his deeds. If he speaks of himself and, like a rotten member, does not exclude himself from his own prayer, we must listen to his actions and the confession of his hands. The true meaning of what he says is: "So, Lord, let Your will be broken in heaven as I break it on earth, so that just as I live against Your commandments, I may enter Your kingdom against the laws of Your justice." He will cry out and say he means no such thing and that we are twisting his words. Then you do not pray sincerely or wholeheartedly. You wish for divine will to be fulfilled in one way but not in another. Justice, but not for your house. He might also respond that he does not recite this prayer because it is too dangerous; instead, he recites others that better suit his purpose and have great virtues without so many drawbacks.

I will not pursue this further, not for lack of material or need to address it, but because time is running short. It seems sufficiently proven that when God judges in the conscience of the wicked, they are convicted within themselves, caught in their own nets. If they deny it, we should pay no heed, for their persistent defense, their heart's anger, their evasive maneuvers, their appeals against judgment, their attempts to avoid it altogether—all these are on our side; do not think they signify anything other than their acknowledgment of guilt.

There remains another, even greater danger, although the previous one suffices. This is the anger many feel when they find themselves defeated, the despair they wish to take as their last resort, thinking they will fare better by further angering God. Then they say: "If this is true, if I have no defense, if the things I do for my own good do not make me a friend of the One who will judge me, and if I cannot use them as an excuse, I resolve to stop doing them. Why should I want them if they do not serve me?" These responses are more common than you think and are also old. Thus the wicked say through Jeremiah (18), to this same end: "It is hopeless; we will continue with our own plans; each of us will follow the stubbornness of his evil heart."

Does it seem to you that this is a good remedy? To despair as a remedy and despair to become worse? Why, being evil, when not regarded as good, resolve to become much worse, and anger God or His Word so greatly, to the extent that, in order to anger Him more and as a form of vengeance, add new evils? Friend, do not say such a thing. It is enough that in the first instance you were like Cain in being blind and stubborn and in attempting to defend yourself against the Lord; do not be like him in the second instance, which is in despair. The worse you think you are, the more you must restrain your heart so that you do not go further. If you were to despair of the false remedy in order to seek the true one, that is what we seek; but to take the liberty to be worse, may God keep us from that. What has been told to you is a great truth and a truth from heaven. But if your sin has you so defeated that you do not want to leave it, do not stop doing the good you can, and as much as you can.

I warn you that there is God's wrath, and there is greater wrath; there are evildoers, and there is a great excess of evildoers. What we have discussed so far concerning your judgment serves many purposes. First, so that you understand the truth of your affairs and do not deceive yourself or be deceived by anyone. Second, so that you know that God wants clean hands and a pure heart, and that, where this is not fulfilled according to the demands of His law, there is no excuse, no remedy, no reward, even if it is of all the goods in the world, that can free us or defend us from the wrath of His judgment, so that we are not overcome and overthrown in it. Third, so that you do not become proud or secure, nor think that with them you make a ledger of expense and receipt with God.

The goods of the righteous would be lost in this way, and would not yours be lost? Be careful that what you claim to do for your benefit is not to your own detriment. In the desperation of the wicked we mentioned, the value of their goods is seen, for in not being accepted by God as their excuse, they immediately want to abandon them and do nothing but evil. This desperation is very secret, very gentle, and dissimulated, but I tell you that many of these hanged men would be found in many houses. This is a bad path, do not follow it. Falling into the judgment of God, defeated and convicted of your evil, do not regret it. It is good if, seeing yourself fallen, you seek to rise. The purpose for which you are overthrown is this. He who had the power to bring you down has the power to lift you up, and with the first He invites you to the second. The Lord is the one who makes the wound and who will bind it: He strikes, and His hands heal (Job 5).

And since we have taught a remedy for the defeated if they want to emerge victorious, and have overthrown the rebels and the obstinate, convicting them through the Divine Word, as they cannot sustain themselves in the judgment of their conscience when the wrath of God judges within it; but are carried away like dust, having no more resistance than it does, let us now say how the righteous remain, remaining secure and strong, like the great and powerful trees when the wind shakes them. The righteous remain uplifted and firm in the judgment we discussed because they have a joyful and peaceful conscience. These are the main weapons with which they resist, very contrary to those of the wicked. The joyful and secure conscience, says Solomon, is like a continuous feast (Proverbs 15). No sorrow or hunger or bitterness intervenes to cause unrest: great is the spirit in love with the goodness of God, and the heart without treachery towards Him. This is our glory, says St. Paul, the testimony of our conscience, that with simplicity and godly sincerity, not with worldly wisdom, but by the grace of God, we have conducted ourselves in the world, and especially towards you (2 Corinthians 1).

In your own conscience, man, you will find the weapons with which you will face death, if you are to face it; and within it, you will also find those that will protect you in God's judgment. How little benefit will come from striving to cast away the bad, if you possess them, as we have already stated; strive instead to possess those which the Lord himself wishes you to use for your defense when he calls you to account. The wicked may now say that we greatly hinder their prideful deeds, yet allow it for the righteous, because this peace and security we seek in conscience seems like a license to become arrogant and to reckon with God as one man does with another. It is necessary for us to respond, for from this will come great clarity in understanding this matter, which holds all the importance and the key to a Christian's salvation. Even Satan disguises himself as an angel of light (2 Corinthians 11), and in place of hope, he instills pride; in place of faith, boldness; and in place of peace, lost dreams.

We have already seen many who have taken lessons and instruction for this holy testimony of conscience and, being very pleased to have found it, later realize that neither their instructors nor they themselves had done anything but open the door to the spirit of vanity, making the path to perdition more insidious and harder to recognize. Christian peace requires Christian mortification; it entails a profound understanding of sin and no pride in one's righteousness. We will say only briefly what pertains to our purpose; the rest will be left for its appropriate place. Saint Paul teaches us all this in a few words. "I care very little if I am judged by you," he says, "or by any human court; indeed, I do not even judge myself. My conscience is clear, but that does not make me innocent" (1 Corinthians 4).

If we reconcile these two statements from the same author, and such an author, the one we just mentioned and the one we cited earlier, that "the testimony of our conscience is our glory," we will have laid the groundwork for understanding what we are discussing. The principal value of all this, what the Christian must strive for and not trade for all the treasures and goods in the world, is to call upon God in truth, invoking Him without any intention of malice, without deceit, with obedience to His commandments, without the determined will to break even one of them, no matter the cost. The wealth of man lies in calling upon God; calling upon Him and being heard consists in ensuring that when he turns his eyes to his heart, he does not find there the enemies of the very Lord he invokes, not seeking to cast them out, but rather sustaining and loving them.

We have already taken one step, which is that God hears those who call upon Him in this way, and He hears them out of His clemency, for so He has promised. It remains that the righteousness of such a man depends on being heard and being answered in the audience of mercy. He does not cry out: "O LORD! Do not bring your servant into judgment, for no living being will be justified in your sight" (Psalm 143). The satisfaction and peace of the just consist in hoping to be judged with mercy. The audience of God's justice is a rigorous matter; where the wicked are judged, there is no defense or refuge for them. They will be overthrown there as they are here; for they themselves are witnesses of how they love their treacheries.

The righteous say: Lord, if I have enmity with my sin, it is because You placed it there; if I have sought to cast it from my heart, it is Your weapons that have done so; if I move forward, You sustain me; if I am tempted, it is born from my own wretchedness; if I am weak, it comes from me; if I am not entirely clean, it is my own hindrance; if there is so much in me that each hour it is necessary for You to intervene, and even with all this I am not cleansed, it is the harvest of my corrupt heart, remnants of my old deeds, testimony of what I would be if You abandoned me. Your Word, Lord, sustains me and gives me hope, so that when I am judged, Your mercy will hear and judge me; when I have nothing to say, You will respond for me; with the blood of Your Son, You will complete what I could not, refine what is rough, cleanse what needs to be more pure, lend to the poor, give to anyone who has, as You have said (Luke 19), fill what is lacking, and show who You are, and the value of what You have given us.

These are the weapons with which the righteous stand firm in the judgment where the wicked fall. These are the defenses of his conscience, the firmness on which he stands; so that, although he is attacked, he is not overcome; although he is shaken, he is not toppled. He does not fall due to despair, nor by resisting with pride, nor by hiding his sin; he stands firm by confession, remains steadfast by hope, because he has his roots planted in the mercy of God.

It remains to discuss the third judgment, by which God also holds account in this world with both the righteous and the wicked, and reveals His justice, and the truth and firmness of His Word. This is when He punishes some and rewards others in this life, sometimes through trials, sometimes through the cross, sometimes by overturning the ways the world had them established, calling men to repentance and testing who belongs to Him and who does not. In this judgment, as in the previous ones, the wicked are carried away like dust, while the righteous stand firm like trees.

There is extensive mention of this manner, in which God often judges, in the prophets. Micah (6) makes a great protest, summoning the mountains and hills and the foundations of the earth to be present at the judgment God wishes to make concerning His people; He disputes with them first, then the threats follow. Isaiah (3) says: The LORD will come to judgment against the elders of His people and their princes. And our Prophet in many places deals with this same judgment (Psalm 10 and 76).

Of all three judgments, the one least understood and believed by the world is this one we are discussing. The prosperity of the wicked seems to last so long that, to attain on earth what the people of the earth desire: wealth, power, honors, advantages, pleasures, and joys, it is already established that the most certain path is that of malice, whether overt or covert; and that to never achieve these things is to follow what we call virtue and being Christians. We could almost come to terms with them if they only had this rule for acquiring, but they say it is even more certain for preserving and advancing. The Divine Scripture threatens the downfall of these and promises prosperity to the righteous, but worldly people care little about believing what it says in this regard; they hold their rule as true, claiming to find it so by experience; these other things must have other interpretations, which they care very little about.

The faith of the righteous adheres to the Word of God, placing all their hope in it. The greed and wisdom of the wicked follow the rule that aligns best with the force and madness of their lost desires. I do not deny that wickedness can achieve many of the vanities that men covet in this life, and that through it they may obtain the wealth and dignities that should rightfully belong to the righteous, were the world just. But I affirm and believe what the Holy Scripture states on this matter: that God takes account of sinners, and at the peak of their negligence and possession of their goods, He cuts the thread and brings them down, dispersing them like dust in the face of the storm. They do not know how or when this will happen, nor do they believe it can happen; but God knows it will happen, and He chooses the time. Despite all his adversity, Job held this view, stating that he knows and is certain that the wicked will be like chaff before the wind, and like stubble that the whirlwind carries away.

In this same judgment, the righteous prosper because, although the ignorance of the wicked may judge them as forgotten and without foundation, in truth, they are the well-planted trees of great strength that stand firm in judgment, while the others are the chaff with no resistance. I began by saying that this matter is one of faith, because only the faithful can understand it; the others remain lost, not comprehending the path of their own destruction. I want to explain this further so that it becomes more apparent how God upholds His truth, and how we must conduct ourselves to avoid being lost by straying from Him. The entire difference lies in the fact that the wicked look no further than the present time; they seek their prosperity in it and lay foundations for the future based on it. What they have in hand is, in their view, the rule for what is to come, believing that one thing will lead to another.

They have no other hope than this, nor more faith than what you have heard, because if they had anything else, they would take a different path for their intentions. But being so short-sighted in understanding God's judgments, they see nothing beyond what is immediately before them and make it the general rule for everything. From the past, they never learn; they neither understand nor acknowledge it, nor do they take it as a lesson in faith or as knowledge of divine truth and justice. If you understand this, you will see clearly that the wicked, who never recognize anything but the present, reduce everything to it and make it the general rule for everything.

The righteous follow a different path: they have hope for other times, knowing that these are in God's hands; for the present, they have patience, with an understanding of their sin; they sustain and strengthen their faith with the memory of the past, attentively considering God's great judgments, the friendship He maintained with His own, and the punishment He inflicted on the wicked. Sinners mock all this, considering it great foolishness; they pay no heed to what has already happened; they do not think they can reach the future, nor do they know how, and if any fear remains in them, they provide for it by adding more wickedness. The present is what they seek; the future does not exist for them, and if it does, it will be, as we have said, guided by what they currently hold.

The first folly of these individuals is to underestimate the power of God and to think that there is a way and a time to escape His hands. The second is like the first, which is to measure in themselves what can hurt them and how much it can hurt, believing that God's hand will not find them where it punishes, except where they provide, and that they are safe from everything else. The third folly is not recognizing through past events the care that the Lord has taken to support His friends and to punish His enemies.

God's wrath has consistently demonstrated significant signs against the wicked and great favor toward the righteous, granting prosperous ends to the latter and disastrous ends to the former. This is evidenced by the fall of Babylon, Nineveh, Egypt, and other great empires of the world; the punishments of numerous tyrants, the ends and fates of many wicked people; and the sudden prosperities of many righteous individuals, guided and favored against all earthly resistance and knowledge. There is no need to look to the distant past: our own times and those of everyone bear witness to this same truth, leaving us without excuse or the pretense of ignorance when God takes account.

However, as our eyes are blinded by great infidelity, infected by our follies, distracted by our vanities, and lifted by our greed and pride, we fail to believe that God's hand has wrought the past and continues to act in the present, nor do we recognize that His justice operates with great attention to execute what His Word declares. We never consider the humble matters where we could see this every day; instead, we fix our eyes on some lofty, grand affairs, where their vanity and rarity further confuse and make us more foolish. Consequently, when punishment comes, it takes us by surprise and unprepared; we are left with the suffering and without the warning, punished but not corrected, wounded without knowing by whose hand or for what purpose.

In conclusion, God's Word asserts that it is certain that the wicked in the judgment of this world and in worldly matters fall and are overthrown, while the righteous are favored and remain steadfast. The sinner finds it very difficult to understand this. Whom shall we trust more? What the Scripture says is not without evidence; rather, the wicked lack the eyes to see it and the judgment to understand it. We said that even in this case there is a separation, like that of trees from chaff and dust. Do we not have great examples of this given for this very purpose and to confirm this great truth? When God wanted to destroy Sodom, did He not send an angel to separate Lot and his household before the fire came? (Genesis 6)

Here the response is ready: a single swallow does not make a summer; these and all that can be discussed are few examples from few eras, and the counterexamples of the wicked whose prosperity continued and who withstood the tempests of the world, and of the righteous who were seemingly consumed and forgotten, are numerous. Their response requires that this not be drawn from our head or imagination, for that would be very vain. Since Sacred Scripture is the teacher of this doctrine, it is reasonable that it itself provides the answer and sheds true light on the path of the faithful, encouraging them for their labor.

Part of this answer has already been given in the little we have said about the examples of God's mercy and wrath, and the fulfillment of His Word; in what we began to declare about the blindness of the wicked in their assessments of the times, and the ways they ensure they never look at what should warn and teach them, but always fix their eyes on what conforms to their appetites and blind desires. From all this, it follows that what is clear seems dark to them; what happens every day appears unprecedented; and conversely, what has fallen seems very exalted; what never had truth seems to be on a very sure path.

The remaining response and the explanation of what we have briefly summarized here will be addressed in the next sermon, where we will continue to discuss this same subject. Firstly, because including everything here would make it excessively long; and secondly, because it is as appropriate to that context as it is to this one. The two verses are interlinked, with each explaining the other, and together they help to clarify the message. What is essential for understanding and benefiting from what has been said is to firmly believe that God knows more about our well-being and our faults than we do. We must trust that what His Word declares in this matter is an unfailing truth. The execution and fulfillment of everything must be entrusted to His infinite wisdom. With great hope and by seeking the Lord's favor, we should strive with all our might to remain steadfast in the judgment of our conscience. By doing so, we can be assured that the One who awaits us in the final judgment to bring us into His company will not forsake us in the trials of this life.

The Sixth Sermon

Porque conoce el Señor el camino de los justos;
y el camino de los malos perecerá.[13]

IN THIS FINAL VERSE, the same theme as previously discussed is continued, presenting the ultimate and concluding reason for everything that has been said. As it is the conclusion of the Psalm, it serves as a culmination and a point of clarity with which David seeks to awaken us and provide comprehensive understanding of the preceding messages, offering it as a refuge and a source of strength for understanding these matters, especially during times of temptation.

We have stated that the wicked do not stand nor hold firm in the judgment of God, whereas the righteous remain upright and steadfast. We discussed three types of judgment, and in each one, we verified the truth of our Prophet's assertion. Now, a reason follows that encompasses everything and reveals the secret and the means by which everything is directed: "For the Lord knows the way of the righteous, but the way of the wicked will perish."

Everything hinges on the favor granted to the righteous and the disfavor the wicked have brought upon themselves through the persistence of their evil deeds. There is nothing that God does not know, nor can anything be hidden from His infinite wisdom. "The LORD knows the thoughts of man, that they are vain" (Psalm 94). "The heart is deceitful above all things,

---

13. "for the Lord knows the way of the righteous, but the way of the wicked will perish" (Ps. 1:6, ESV).

and desperately wicked; who can know it? I, the LORD, search the heart, I test the mind" (Jeremiah 17).

However, the term "know" in the Divine Scripture is often understood to mean "approve" and "favor." The foolish virgins are answered in the Gospel: "Truly I say to you, I do not know you" (Matthew 25). Through the prophet Amos (3), God says to the people of Israel: "You only have I known of all the families of the earth." In these and many other passages that could be cited, it is clear what is meant by "know." In our verse, it is as if it said: God favors the way of the righteous and takes care of it, while the way of the wicked is unfavored.

Thus, it is settled that the statement made by David in the conclusion of the Psalm, expressed in clearer terms for us, is as follows: "Because the Lord is in charge of the way, the outcomes, and the ends of the righteous; and the matters of the wicked, being abandoned and left to their own devices, will come to a bad end." This is the cause, and none can deny it. No one with any sense will dispute that one will fare well whom God favors and takes charge of their affairs, and that one is on a bad path whom God abandons.

It remains for us to demonstrate the certainty that God indeed acts in both ways: as the protector of the righteous and their affairs, and as the adversary of the wicked and their endeavors. If the sinner were to acknowledge both truths and genuinely accept them, he would immediately abandon his sinful life and misguided thoughts; but he is unwilling to recognize this, and if he were to admit anything, it would be the first point: that those under God's vigilant care are truly secure, and those whom He pursues are without remedy. He will, however, deny the second point: that the Lord acts in such a manner toward the one and in such a way toward the other.

We have already discussed how sinners deny and acknowledge these truths; it remains for us to prove what has been proposed.

The arguments that the wicked have for not believing that God is so opposed to them and so in favor of the righteous are substantial. These arguments are so compelling that they place even the righteous in great distress, and they openly admit that this is the most severe temptation they face, among many others that cause them anguish in this life. Let us not spend too much time on the various passages from Sacred Scripture that could be cited; one example from our Prophet will suffice, where it is quite clear what we mean. "My feet had almost slipped; I had nearly lost my foothold. For I envied the arrogant when I saw the prosperity of the wicked" (Psalm 73).

If such understanding troubled so great a saint, such a close friend of God, who knew so much of His secrets, what effect will it have on those who are far from such perfection? And if it combats all types of the righteous, both more perfect and less perfect, so intensely, where will the blind and the lost stand, who find no pleasure in other goods except those of this world? The righteous are not so much troubled for themselves as they are for others. Each is prepared to bear his cross, but it is the charity and concern for his neighbor that cause great distress. The wicked love themselves so blindly that they have an unrestrained desire to possess everything for themselves, from which it can easily be inferred how devoid of judgment they will be in considering what we are discussing.

Since the argument is so strong, it must be true that great prosperity and satisfaction are often achieved through wickedness, and that the majority of those prospering and content in this world are wicked; for if it were otherwise, this temptation would not be so severe for the righteous, nor would sinners follow this wicked path so widely to fulfill their desires.

Now it remains to prove the truth of what the Prophet and the Holy Spirit say: that God is in charge of the way of the righteous and that the way of the wicked will perish, while also responding to the contradiction that has been posed. It is well to begin with what is least esteemed, which is spiritual prosperity, the goods of the soul, its goodness and justice, through which it is to achieve perpetual and blessed life. After this, we will speak of the other aspects that matter more, if we heed the judgment of the world: lives, possessions, honors, tyrannies, debaucheries, delights, pleasures, and, to sum it up in one word, such brutalities.

If our discussion were solely with the wicked, we could easily dispense with the first point, because, whether clearly or hesitantly, they would eventually admit that the goods of the other life are acquired through goodness and justice. However, they persist in the belief that the path for the wealthy is shorter and more certain, which will be addressed elsewhere. But since we must consider the righteous and those striving to be so, it is fitting to dwell a little longer on this point, to confirm them in the truth and help them recognize God's care for their salvation, so they may appreciate and serve Him.

In Scripture, and in daily life, there are righteous individuals who falter, are overcome, and fall away from the great friendship they had with the Lord. During their fall, and while they are fallen, they lose the name of righteous. Strictly speaking, this name no longer suits them. If they are called righteous, it refers to the long time they were righteous before, and the long time they will be righteous afterward, with only a brief period in sin, from which they deeply repent and emerge with great learning. God has special care to rescue such individuals from sin: they are His chosen ones. He knows they were very faithful to Him, recognizes that they will be again, powerfully awakens them, chastises them with a rigorous hand, and opens great paths for their remedy. We see examples of this in David, in Saint Peter, and in a great multitude of saints.

I do not know how to emphasize this more than by what is said in the Book of Wisdom, which states that God often takes His own in early age and without apparent reason to men, so they are not harmed by remaining in this world. "He was taken away lest wickedness should alter his understanding or deceit beguile his soul" (Wisdom 4). Is there any understanding, Lord, that can comprehend Your diligence and the mercy You show to Your own? Like a wise gardener, You gather the fruit early so that time does not spoil it. Is there anything that can match this? Through the prophet Hosea (2), God threatens His people, saying, "Therefore I will block her path with thornbushes; I will wall her in so that she cannot find her way."

If in what seems to be punishments and scourges from His hand, there is such great favor hidden, if in what initially tastes bitter, there are such sweet elements mixed in, what will there be in His manifest favors and clear gifts? This is the way and the means by which God treats His own; these are His actions. Consider what the rest must be like. As for the sinners, does He not seek them, call them, lest they be lost? Indeed, He does. But just as by righteous we mean one who, if fallen, felt his fall, wept over his perdition, and took advantage of favor to leave that evil path and return to his former state, so by sinner and wicked we mean one who loves his perdition, who wants to remain in it, who seeks excuses and distractions, who, when given a hand, stays put, when lifted up, lets himself fall, when illuminated with light, closes his eyes, when called, does not want to hear.

To such individuals, divine justice often grants a favor that the world calls favors, the kind that sinners themselves desire, the kind they ask for in their prayers and sacrifices, so they cannot claim deception. The path they want smooth, He leaves smooth for them; they do not wish to find a cross on it, as it is a bad omen to them, akin to the gallows, not so much due to the hardness of their hearts: they walked in their own counsels. Through Hosea (4), He threatens that He will not punish or castigate their daughters when they sin, but will give them room to shamelessly indulge in their looseness.

And it is the ultimate punishment that can befall them in this world: these are the favors the wicked seek, the happiness they so desire, this is what they ask of God, and for this very reason, they deny Him. They consider it a great good; Divine Scripture counts it as a great punishment. In the scourging and the cross of the righteous, we said that great gentleness and great comfort were hidden; in the prosperity of sinners, the Lord affirms that a concealed poison, the most dangerous and harmful imaginable, comes with it.

If discussing this with people who have some understanding of true good and true evil, what we have said would suffice to establish as certain and verified: the righteous prospering in all things in this world, with God taking care of all their affairs; and the path of the wicked being entirely unfavored, with no success in anything. If trials and adversities are a great opportunity for some to avoid being lost in this life and to attain the one that has no end, and the rest and abundance of false goods blind others so they sleep and daily forget more and entangle themselves further in their perdition, what reason could support labeling the former as misfortune or disfavour, and the latter as prosperity or good? Who would be so foolish as to judge as a bad deed the actions of a wise doctor administering initially bitter-tasting but very effective medicines for the patient's health? And as a good deed the actions of a foolish mother who, in indulging her child, gives him everything he wants?

But because it seems too much to discuss this with them, and the stubbornness of their foolishness and desires, along with their discussions about it, testify to how they understand and believe it, we will leave it for now with what has been said and address these goods of theirs, in which their hearts are so invested and through which their obstinacy measures favor and disfavor, good and bad in this world. I say then that, speaking in the sense in which they understand this matter, the wicked are prospered in this life and brought down and treated as who they are.

They are alarmed by such a harsh sentence because it seems to them that everything is at stake here, that of the other, you would care little. And so that you do not comfort yourselves by thinking that this is my imagination and therefore something vain, I want you to know that it is something God says, and the decree of His justice. To remove all stumbling blocks and any occasion for error from the good, it is good for them to know first that what we now affirm does not cast out the cross that the Gospel and all of Scripture announce to those who wish to follow the truth; at the same time, the cross is borne, and great prosperity is attained, and poverty and dishonor and trials and death of the first do not hinder the second.

The world's judgment does not understand how this can be reconciled, but faith attains it, and understands that it is a very certain matter, as we will later prove. Let us begin with the most evident, proving with examples that what we have said is a great truth. They cannot deny the favors that God showed to Abraham, Jacob, Job, and many others, as we mentioned in previous sermons; nor can they deny the downfalls of Pharaoh, Nebuchadnezzar, Sennacherib, and countless others. It was clearly demonstrated in these cases how divine justice wants to take away from the wicked the possession of the goods they value and for which they are wicked. Here, He wants to punish them in what hurts them most and make them pay for the great evils they committed against the righteous. He also wants to protect the righteous, delivering them from the tyranny of sinners, showing them, and giving them evidence of what He has prepared for them in heaven, as He does not leave them without a share of earthly things. The examples are not as few as the wicked respond, nor are those they allege on their part so many; rather, it is entirely the reverse—they do not have even one example to undo what the Divine Word says in this case, and the examples we have to confirm its great truth are innumerable.

Now it is appropriate to declare what we have sometimes hinted at, that the knowledge and judgment of this is a matter of faith, and that only faith understands it, and the blindness of the wicked does not qualify them to speak of it. God does not fulfill His truth according to the appetite and fickleness of the flesh, because it is neither reasonable for Him to be bound by the judgment and opinion of such a foolish thing, nor for the artifice of His great justice to be undone, nor the wonders of His mercy, nor for the test of the righteous to be hindered, nor the examination and purification of good works, nor the great deeds of those who serve Him, nor the confusion of the wicked. All this would happen in reverse if every time one did a good deed, they became rich, honored, freed from all dangers and troubles, and conversely, if the wicked immediately became poor, received a thousand affronts, were cast out of the world, and everything went wrong for them.

Many have demanded this rule and this path from God, and because they did not find it as certain and palpable as they wanted, they fell into great delusions and lost opinions. To understand this, it is necessary to know the sin that reigned over men, the wrath that God shows against it, the state of penance and exile in which we live, and the cross to which the just and the unjust are subject. Consideration must be given to the need we have to be punished, to have a curb on our appetites, to be kept away from occasions of loss, and to undergo continuous mortification for the remnants of our sin. It should also be considered the vigilance of the devil against us, and how the greatest entry he could have would be the great security and neglect with which our pride would be directed.

No one should think that our sinful nature is so easily swayed that all these interests alone would prevent us from sinning as we know Adam did. Above all, God desires that His followers be tested, and that true faith be the means through which they experience His merciful works, while the infidelity and rebellion of the wicked justify the justice by which they are punished. Therefore, when the righteous see the examples we have mentioned, they judge and measure them with their faith: they know that God is true and leave the manner of His truth's fulfillment to Him.

The wicked are blind to this judgment and thus walk toward their perdition without understanding where or how they are going until they find themselves lost. The people of Sodom were far from thinking that the guests Lot took into his house were angels who came to save him from the fire that would descend upon the city. In the end, he was saved, and they were killed, becoming a perpetual example of God's great wrath (Genesis 19).

To better understand and more easily remember this, we will follow this order: we will confirm the statement of our Psalm with others from Scripture, for as it is of one spirit, there is no contradiction in it, only great harmony; and then we will continue what we began, explaining how the righteous understand it and how the wicked understand it, for everything depends on this.

Let us first speak of the favor shown to the righteous, as our verse places them first and says that God knows their way and takes care of it. We will then discuss the sinners and the wrong path they follow. In many other places, David says the same as here, because, being of such great importance, he repeats it often. "The steps of a good man are ordered by the LORD, and He delights in his way. Though he fall, he shall not be utterly cast down, for the LORD upholds him with His hand" (Psalm 37). In this way, the disasters that befall the righteous in this life are like falls from which they are caught by the powerful and merciful hand of God, from which it clearly follows that little harm comes from the fall, and they will be lifted up again at the best time. Solomon says: "He who follows righteousness and mercy finds life, righteousness, and honor" (Proverbs 21). "He who fears the LORD will not suffer harm; in the midst of temptation, God will preserve him and deliver him from all" (Ecclesiasticus 33).

No need to cite more authorities, as these will suffice for some, and nothing will suffice for others. Let us now address the wicked and compare them to the righteous. "I have seen the wicked in great power, spreading himself like a green tree in its native soil. Yet he passed away, and behold, he was no more; I sought him, but he could not be found" (Psalm 37). "The curse of the LORD is on the house of the wicked, but He blesses the dwelling of the righteous" (Proverbs 3).

Now it remains to shed light and clarity on all this, to discuss how these principles apply to the righteous and how they apply to the wicked, how each understands these principles, to explain many reasons that were touched upon lightly in this and the previous sermon, and to elaborate on them intentionally here.

We have already mentioned the subjection we have in this world to endure the cross, the reason for this, and the benefits that accrue to us. This is the principal foundation for the righteous and the greatest light for all their affairs. The righteous understand that they need restraint and that they deserve punishment. They comprehend that everything is guided by the hand of God, and that His principal aim is mercy and favor for those who turn to Him and do not wish to be lost. From this results great patience and resistance to temptation; they do not abandon the law of the Lord but rather embrace it as their remedy. They mix all their trials with a joy and hope that all will have a prosperous end because the hand that sends these trials is prepared and powerful to bestow innumerable rewards and favors.

The wicked, however, have a different understanding of all this; they find no satisfaction, no benefit, no good end in adversities. They claim that everything is guided by the hand of God, but they say and feel this as coldly as their actions reveal. The satisfaction of their desires, no matter how abominable, fills them so completely that they cannot believe it comes from the hand of the devil, but rather see it as good fortune. Crosses and tribulations are not seen as sent by God but as guided by the devil. Observe how corrupted their sense is by their wicked desires. The wicked cannot deny this; their own words reveal it. When troubles come, you will hear nothing but curses and oaths; when their evil desires are fulfilled and they are ensnared in their own traps, they praise God for directing them and entrust Him with their future. In this view, they immediately switch to another extreme, attributing the good they enjoy to the devil and the bad to God; consider whom they serve and whose paths they follow for everything else.

From this initial difference between the righteous and the sinner, another follows among the same individuals. The righteous immediately recognize prosperity and benefit from it, even when it comes accompanied by countless trials and crosses; the wicked cannot recognize it unless it is given clean and free of all trouble. The one has the vision to recognize it, while the other sees through such false and deceitful lenses that they can only perceive very grand things.

The righteous measure favor with a measure that comes full and overflows; they measure it with repentance and with the cross that they know their sins deserve; they measure it with the mercy of God, understanding what He does; they measure it with the hope that the same Lord who gives now will provide for the future, as He remains as powerful, wise, merciful, and providential as ever. With this measure, Tobit (4) said to his son: "Do not be afraid, my son; we live a poor life, but we will have many good things if we fear God." With this measure, St. Paul wrote to Timothy: "Godliness with contentment is great gain. For we brought nothing into this world, and it is certain we can carry nothing out. So, having food and clothing, let us be content with these" (1 Timothy 6).

If we look at the pleasures of the righteous, they are also in great abundance; for the mere understanding of God's works brings such great contentment that no power in the world can take it away. Rest brings joy; work brings joy as well: in both, they know they are in the hands of such a Lord that no greater good can be asked or desired in this world. Wherever their thoughts and faith may roam, they recognize divine wisdom, goodness, power, and mercy. They know they are redeemed from their sin, heirs to great goods, and preserved for the great glory of the One who freed them. They humble themselves with caution about their own weaknesses, ask for favor to avoid losing themselves, and this hope brings them joy, making them sleep and wake with it. Ultimately, those who love God cannot lack immense contentment; for it is enough to know who they love, how great and powerful He is, how rich in infinite goods, how certain it is that He will never diminish, how well-placed their love is in Him, how right it is to serve Him, how sure they are of being loved in return, of partaking in His goods, and of being in His company without being able to be separated from it.

Imagine that in some love, like that of a mother for her child, a small imitation of these things could be achieved, and consider the great pleasure that would result for such a mother. Then reflect on the circumstances that exist in this other kind of love for the pleasure of those who love. While the man lives in this world, he mixes with great hardships; but none can be so great as to deprive the good of their joy. The flesh feels the burden as its own dwelling place; but it cannot conquer the strength and virtue of the spirit.

We have discussed how the righteous measure their prosperity and pleasures, and we have found them to be very wealthy; now let's speak of the sinner and you will see how blind he is. The sinner measures with a bottomless measure; consider when a bottomless thing can be filled or when the one measuring with it can be satisfied. He measures with his pride, with his ambition, with his envy, with his tyranny, with his madness and blindness, and with the never-ending thought that there will be no end.

Everything we have said is true, and if you do not believe it, let's ask him. Why do you want so much wealth, man? Why do you amass so much? Is your stature greater than that of others? Why do you, without regard for the laws of God or those of men, want to grasp everything? If we measure by your needs, you have more than enough. With what do you measure? The only answer is that he measures with his pride. Does it have a bottom? It has no bottom. Do you want to see that this is so? Reason will tell you. How would you know that a vessel lacks a bottom? You would know if, when pouring water or another substance into it, no matter how much you pour, it never fills up or bulges, but you keep pouring and it remains empty.

The pride of the sinner declares that against God and against justice, it always wants to advance; the more it has, the less content it becomes. It can hold more now than before, and the more you pour in, the more it can hold. Therefore, does it not have a bottom? Indeed, it is so. If what should make it diminish makes it grow, if what should satisfy it makes it hungrier, if what should quench it ignites it, it has no bottom. So who can satisfy this man? No one, since not even everything God created in this world can suffice; because, even if it were all his, he would still want more, given his inherent faults. For the strength and understanding he has, what he has in hand is more than sufficient. For the measure of his ambition, all the world's business and dealings are very narrow. For governing himself, he lacks enough understanding; but for what his tyranny demands, he would gladly take on the responsibility of ruling everything on earth. What he needs has an end, regardless of how long his life may be, but since he measures not by this but by his envy, everything that seems good in others' houses, he wants to bring into his own, and he wants everything else to diminish so that his possessions appear greater. Thus, if his pride, ambition, tyranny, and envy have no limit, and with this he wants to measure everything, when will this man be satisfied?

It goes even further: not only does he want to measure his interests with his madness, but he also wants to measure them with the madness of others. He persistently tries to awaken envy in all his neighbors, on one hand, and to satisfy the vanities of others' eyes and the plots and the pleasures of their follies, on the other. Foolish man, who not only wants to follow the whims of your own madness but also works and toils to become a scarecrow for mine! We could tolerate if this man only wanted to measure his own things with measures that have no bottom, but he also wants to measure with the same measures the poor fellow in his corner, content with the state and condition God has placed him in. Suffice it, wicked man, to measure your interests and your pleasures with your pride, ambition, and folly; let the other measure his fate and his pleasures with his heart. For the purpose with which he has gauged it, he is rich; for the joy God has given him, he has enough to be happy.

Your measures have no bottom, who made you so tyrannical that you enter another's house to measure their interests?

Not everything that your pride and envy encompasses stops or takes shape within them, yet you want it to appear as it does in your neighbor's possessions. If you did not measure what the other person achieves with these measures, you would not think so little of it, nor would you trample it so much, nor would you hate the path they follow so extremely, nor would you distance yourself so much from God to distance yourself from it. You find contentment only in imitating beasts; your palate is only satisfied with the indulgence and perverseness that your body demands, and yet you insist on measuring what God wants to place in the other's heart in the same way? You imagine that all the goods in the world are little for someone like you. The other person has such great knowledge of their sins that all the sufferings of this life seem very light for what their faults deserve.

You have seen the first difference between the righteous and the sinner, which is so great and manifest that it is not surprising if it produces various effects and very different satisfactions in them. One has charity, the other has envy; one knows that what is given to them is not just for themselves, but also to share with their brother; the other wishes that what belongs to everyone was only for themselves; one has humility, the other has pride; one thinks daily of death and the end of the journey, the other never thinks they will die. One has God as a judge, the other wants to satisfy the judgment of the world's madness. One has their spirit attuned to the taste of holy pleasures, the other knows no other good than what their senses can experience. One has endurance for trials, awakening patience and repentance for sins; the other ignites in anger and seeks to remedy it by adding more treachery. One measures themselves by what they are and what suffices for what they are; the other measures by what is neither what they are nor what is possible to be.

This is the summary of the difference, so you can understand it better with this brief recap. Herein lies the reason why the sinner deceives himself when he asserts that there are very few good people whom God greatly favors in this world. If measured by his standards, he speaks the truth; there is neither good nor bad whom God favors as he imagines and desires. But if we take the measure of truth, of what is sufficient and necessary, of what will give us true rest, leave our heart free for true goods, and remove the occasions of infinite evils, we will find that the corners of the world are filled with these favored ones of God, while the wicked remain mocked, gluttons and hungry, envious and tormented, exalted and miserable, grasping and discontent, proud and empty, tyrants and fearful, weakened by their delights, and corroded and shamed by the ugliness and baseness of their vileness.

Let us move on to the disfavor of sinners and discuss, as promised, how they are punished and overthrown in this world, and how this is evident to those who have the light of faith, in which declaration the other differences between them and the righteous will be justly spoken of. They reign for a time and flourish with the vain imagination of themselves and those who look at them, but their day is prepared to make evident proof of how despised they are by God. When my day comes, says the Lord through our Prophet, I will judge rightly (Psalm 75).

Sinners in this world resemble corrupt ministers of justice, who never think there will be a reckoning, and if there is, they believe they will soon settle with whoever holds them accountable, because that person will be just like them. God says that when the time comes, He will personally remedy the situation against them. "For the scepter of wickedness shall not rest on the land allotted to the righteous, lest the righteous stretch out their hands to do wrong" (Psalm 125).

As the Divine Word affirms, so it is enacted. Just as we proved that many righteous are protected and favored, it is equally certain that many wicked are overthrown, and indeed, all of them are. In the first case, the wicked are deceived because they measure with poor and false measures; in the second, we have already explained how they are deceived, because they lack faith in the past, present, and future. If these sinners had such faith, or if they were not so deluded by the dreams of their desires, it would be impossible for them not to see clearly what the hand of God has done to all the wicked of the world, in all times and all ages. What memory can they point to of people of this kind that does not immediately highlight their downfall and punishment? Although, as the Prophet says, others have succeeded them in their place (Baruch 3), is the hand of the Lord any less powerful now than it was then? Is He more tolerant and satisfied with wickedness? Have the laws of His justice changed? Does He love the righteous any less? Those examples serve for all others.

The response of the wicked has already begun to be addressed, and now we will put it more plainly. God punishes the wicked collectively, but not individually; He punishes some so that others may take warning and have fear. His justice arrives in due time, but in between, those who fall in the middle escape. Well that may be, but it leaves you living in doubt and anxiety, wondering if you will be among the warned or the examples. Secondly, even if it does not happen in your days, but you die in your false peace, who has assured you that it will not come after your death? This may seem like utter foolishness.

Live as you wish and die without your world crumbling, but let whatever comes after death come at the right time.

You seem to want to imply that you only care about life, and that after it is over, there is neither wine nor anything else to worry about. But we understand it quite differently here, and that you dream of something beyond death. This is evident from the vanities of your legacies, your succession, and your lineage, for which you have spread and continue to spread your nets so widely. And since not all fools err in the same way, it is fitting for all to know that what they think will not matter after death—feeling pain for what did not pain them in life—will indeed matter very much.

Did we not say in the last sermon that one of the follies of sinners is to dictate to God the time when He should punish them, the manner, the how, and the place where it should hurt? You are in a bad place, sinner, if you think time can deliver you from the hands of God. If you do not know where it will hurt, He certainly does; if you understand only one way, He understands many.

The sinner might argue that indeed, a sinner who departs this world without true repentance will be punished for what he has done; but how can he feel pain for what happens here in this age after his departure? He believes that he will pay once and have no further reckoning. Answer yourself, sinner, that you are not in a position to set limits on God's punishment, and that your affairs will be handled in such a way that they will hurt you as much as if you were alive, and even more so. No matter how many accounts you settle and unsettle, no matter how many times you pass through them, do not think that the torments[14] of your misfortune or the news of your per-

---

14. In the Spanish text, the word used is *adehala*, from Arabic, meaning

dition will end so soon. Things will happen here after your departure that will renew a thousand times the wounds of your greed, your pride, your theft, your envy, and your vile and foolish pleasures.

It is not in vain that the wicked are so threatened in the Divine Scripture, with how their plans will be reversed, and how much torment they will suffer in the other world from the things they leave in this one. Do you not remember the rich miser, how the wretch negotiates, and negotiates so vainly, that he sends to his brothers some dead or some visions, so that they do not go where he is? (Luke 16). He sees very well there, only he sees it very late, that he still has much of his pay to receive.

In conclusion, I say and declare what I have said, that the wicked are punished in their very prosperities and pleasures, either clearly in this life or in the things of this life and by the path they feared the most—the loss and disaster of these things, even if they last until death. All this is accounted for, and if it seems otherwise to him, let him wait for the time when everything will be verified, and he will understand who speaks the truth. Some sinners appear more miserable in this life than others, despite being equal in wickedness; but believe me, or believe God, there is a way to equalize them in the very things that seem so unequal to you. This is the conclusion our Prophet gives, responding to the same argument he posed about the good fortune of this wicked people: "My heart was grieved, and I was pricked in my reins. So foolish was I, and ignorant: I was as a beast before thee. Nevertheless, I am continually with thee: thou hast holden me by my right hand. Thou shalt guide

---

"what is given as a bonus over the price of what is bought, sold, or leased. What is added as perks or emoluments to the salary of a job or commission."

me with thy counsel, and afterward receive me to glory" (Psalm 73).

If sinners had judgment, they would see how true and clear the sentence we proposed is, that no matter what happens to them, they are simultaneously prospered in this life and then overthrown and dispossessed of their very goods, and that their very fear takes them away, their own hunger strips them of these, and their very fulfillment is like fuel to the fire, to burn and inflame them more, and to increase their thirst. Look at the uneasy sleep their guilty conscience gives them at the best of times, no matter how hard they try to defend and numb it, and you will see how much it leaves them to their possessions. The very pleasures for which they are lost disgrace them in their hearts, and they wish to hide them from the world; such is their self-awareness, leaving above all the account that will be taken of them later.

How different it is for the righteous, how great is their prosperity in this life, with the hope they have in God; how many possessions and good news they receive daily from the fulfillment of their righteous desires and the very goods here after they have departed! But how could this not be true, with God in charge of all their affairs? He entrusted the times to the same Lord who governs them and has them all present. How could He lack time?

A single remedy remains for the sinner: to return to God with true repentance. No matter how much he is an enemy, he is being awaited; no matter how far he has strayed, he will not lack favor to find himself near. Let him propose within himself that the Lord created and seeks him to make him blessed and rich with inestimable goods. What is the path? To avoid evil counsel, the way of sinners, and the seat of scoffers. He should consider well and see how the Lord would deny him the little, and what is given to many, if He does not deny him such great and privileged things as the kingdom of heaven, being a child of God, and the blood of the Redeemer of the world, to guide him to these things.

If he properly understands his own works and defects, they will disillusion him and tell him that it is safer and better suited to the way of the cross. For everything, God's law will give him strength and light. Let him place this in his heart as a treasure, where lies the esteem and value of all goods, and greater goods than man can conceive. Here he will find all the riches he desires, free from all scruples and torments of a guilty conscience, not sought or begged for in the scarcity and misery of the world, not in fear of fortune or its changes, not ended by brief years. God's word alone created and governs all, given to one who loves so much that He gave His own Son for him, deposited in His promises, which would not fail even if heaven and earth fail, but which is upheld by His power, against which no one can resist.

Here he will find pleasures without the decay of ugliness and without a mix of defects or bitterness; here, wisdom that cannot be lost or deceived. He will be like a tree planted by streams of perpetual waters, which, no matter how much contradiction the world and the entire kingdom of the devil bring against it, can never be moved, nor will it be hindered from bearing fruit in its season, because the Lord of all times is in charge of all its affairs, and will preserve and make it prosper, so that it may reign with Him forever without end. Amen.

Constantino Ponce de la Fuente

CONSTANTINO PONCE DE LA FUENTE (1502-1560), also known as Dr. Constantino, was born in San Clemente, in the province of Cuenca. He received a theological education at the Universidad de Alcalá and fulfilled most of his ministerial work in Seville, arriving there in 1533. He was the chief preacher of the Cathedral, popular with the people and honoured for his writings. At the time of his ministerial service, Seville had become the central point for the Spanish protestant reformation movement. Several theologians, recognized by the Roman Catholic Church, were protestant sympathizers, but it would later be revealed that Dr. Constantino was not just a sympathizer but a covert protestant himself. From 1548 to 1553, Dr. Constantino served as the King's chaplain, earning high respect for his moving sermons, but after his service he returned to Seville where he would continue to minister. Dr. Constantino had already been under suspicion for Lutheranism given his writings, but it was never explicit enough to warrant his arrest. Nonetheless, he was eventually arrested and interrogated by the Spanish Inquisition, and was kept in prison while they sought evidence to condemn his person. While Dr. Constantino continued to affirm his catholicity, it was not until they found his protestant writings, hidden in a secret library of a lady's home, a friend of Dr. Constantino, that he was confronted with the truth. He had written explicitly protestant books and tracts and went through the trouble of hiding it all; there was no more denying it. Upon this discovery, Dr. Constantino confessed to being a protestant and could offer no defense, neither did he recant, for he insisted on keeping true to his protestant convictions. Before he could be executed, however, as other protestants were, he died of illness while incarcerated. This did not prevent the Inquisition from burning his bodily remains as they did for other heretics. While Dr. Constantino may have suffered a lowly death, he was a great spiritual giant in the land of the reformers, a true martyr in the church of Christ.

Scriptural Index

ABOUT THE CÁNTARO INSTITUTE

Inheriting, Informing, Inspiring

The Cántaro Institute is a reformed evangelical organization committed to the advancement of the Christian worldview for the reformation and renewal of the church and culture.

We believe that as the Christian church returns to the fount of Scripture as her ultimate authority for all knowing and living, and wisely applies God's truth to every aspect of life, her missiological activity will result in not only the renewal of the human person but also the reformation of culture, an inevitable result when the true scope and nature of the gospel is made known and applied.